JOSEPH SMITH
THE PROPHET OF THE RESTORATION

JOSEPH SMITH
THE PROPHET OF THE RESTORATION

BY W. JEFFREY MARSH

CFI
SPRINGVILLE, UTAH

ISBN: 1-55517-892-8
v.1

Published by CFI,
an imprint of Cedar Fort, Inc.
925 N. Main, Springville, Utah, 84663
www.cedarfort.com

Distributed by:

Cover painting by Liz Lemon Swindle
Cover design by Nicole Williams
Cover design © 2005 by Lyle Mortimer

Printed in the United States of America
10 9 8 7 6 5 4 3 2 1

Printed on acid-free paper.

CONTENTS

Prologue: Joseph Smith—The Prophet of the
Restoration..IX

1. The Restoration of Light and Truth 1

2. "A Marvelous Work and a Wonder"..........................13

3. Personality of the Prophet 25

4. The Restoration of the Gospel Came
   through, Not from, the Prophet Joseph Smith............41

5. The Education of the Prophet....................................59

6. First Evidence for the Reality of the Restoration:
   Others, Besides Joseph Smith, Received Spiritual
   Confirmations and Personal Winesses from the Spirit 69

7. Second Evidence for the Reality of the Restoration:
   The Prophet Joseph Smith's Mission Was Foreknown
   and Foretold... 77

8. Third Evidence for the Reality of the Restoration:
   The Events of the Restoration Were Foreseen by
   Ancient Prophets 87

9. Fourth Evidence for the Reality of the Restoration:
   The Translation and Restoration of Scripture................. 97

10. Fifth Evidence for the Reality of the Restoration:
    The Restoration of True Doctrine
    and the Plan of Salvation 109

11. Sixth Evidence for the Reality of the Restoration:
    The Restoration of the Savior's Church........................ 119

Epilogue: "Praise to the Man".......................................131

Index 139

JOSEPH SMITH—THE PROPHET OF THE RESTORATION

If a man is measured by how much good he did during his lifetime for the benefit of others, then what are we to think of one whose works increasingly continue to bless people two hundred years after his death? December 23, 2005, marks the bicentennial of the Prophet Joseph Smith's birth. Two centuries have since come and gone, making this an appropriate time to reflect on his life, ministry, and contributions—or better stated—an appropriate time to contemplate the blessings restored by the Lord to the earth for the benefit of all mankind, through His chosen servant, the Prophet Joseph Smith.

All presidents of The Church of Jesus Christ of Latter-day Saints have been and are prophets. But the title "The Prophet" is uniquely reserved for the Prophet Joseph Smith because he was called of God to inaugurate the final gospel dispensation—the dispensation of the fullness of all times. Ancient prophets knew of Joseph Smith's mission and were shown in vision the great work he would do. They bore witness of the gathering of Israel and of the winding up scenes preceding the second coming of Jesus Christ to the earth. Joseph Smith was the one foreordained to set this work in motion and to initiate the events that would culminate in the fulfillment of all these other prophecies.

Truly, Joseph Smith is one of the most preeminent men to ever be born and the foremost theologian to ever step on stage in the world of religion. No one has been his equal. He lived an extraordinary and epic life. His own grandfather Asael Smith once declared that it had been made known to him that "God was going to raise up some branch of his family to be a great benefit to mankind" who would revolutionize the world of religion and herald in a new religious age.[1] Years later, in 1830, Asael's son Joseph Smith Sr. gave him a copy of the recently published Book of Mormon, which he read and fully believed was true. Joseph Smith wrote, "My grandfather . . . long ago predicted that there would be a prophet raised up in his family, and my grandmother was fully satisfied that it was fulfilled in me. My grandfather Asael died [in the fall of 1830] . . . after having received the Book of Mormon, and read it nearly through; and he declared that I was the very Prophet that he had long known would come in his family."[2]

Joseph Smith's contributions to the world of religion are immeasurable because they are never ending. Millions continue to bear witness that Joseph's life and teachings have had a lasting and positive influence in their lives. As John Taylor noted, "Joseph Smith, the Prophet and Seer of the Lord, has done more, save Jesus only, for the salvation of men in this world, than any other man that ever lived in it" (D&C 135:3). When we consider such venerated prophets in the scriptures as Adam, Enoch, Noah, Abraham, and Moses, John Taylor's appraisal of the Prophet Joseph Smith is all the more impressive.

President Harold B. Lee once expressed the desire that all could hear and know about the Prophet Joseph Smith's work. He said, "I remember the prophetic pronouncement that was made from this stand by President George Albert Smith . . . when he said: 'Many have belittled Joseph Smith, and those who have will be forgotten in the remains of mother earth, . . . but [the] honor, majesty, and fidelity to God, attached to Joseph Smith's name and exemplified by him, will never die.'"[3] President Lee insightfully added, "No truer words were ever spoken,"[4] and "I wish that statement could be heard to all the ends of the earth."[5]

As we approach the two hundredth anniversary of Joseph Smith's birth, it is important to look back at the man, as well as his calling. Numerous books have been written about Joseph Smith's life and teachings, but this book, *Joseph Smith—The Prophet of the Restoration*, focuses on his divinely appointed role as the Restorer.

We praise and worship Jesus Christ, our Lord and Savior, for His atoning sacrifice, for His continued concern for us, and for revealing Himself to Joseph Smith. Gratefully, we honor Joseph Smith for his role in the Restoration and testify that all the scriptures that Joseph Smith brought forth bear witness that Jesus Christ is "the only name which shall be given under heaven, whereby salvation shall come unto the children of men" (Moses 6:52; see also Mosiah 3:17). Our testimony to the world is that the Redeemer of all mankind has appeared in our day and called Joseph Smith to restore His gospel—the gospel of Jesus Christ—to the earth one last time. Jesus *is* the Christ, and Joseph *is* the Prophet of the Restoration.

REFLECTING ON THE PAST WITH GRATITUDE

The year 2005 marks several significant anniversaries regarding the restoration of light and truth to the earth. One hundred and eighty-five years ago, in the spring of 1820, the Prophet Joseph Smith experienced his First Vision when God the Eternal Father and His Son Jesus Christ appeared to him in Palmyra, New York, ushering in the final dispensation of the fullness of all times (see Acts 3:19–21). Beginning with that vision and continuing through the remainder of his life, the Prophet Joseph Smith was divinely directed to restore the Church of Jesus Christ, the doctrines of the eternal plan of salvation for all mankind, and the priesthood authority to perform the necessary ordinances for exaltation in the highest degree of glory where God and Christ dwell. Joseph Smith's ministry saw many landmark events that now, in 2005, we look back on with gratefulness. They include the 200th anniversary of the birth of the Prophet Joseph Smith (born December 23, 1805), the 175th anniversary of the printing of the Book of Mormon (first published March 26, 1830), the founding of The Church of Jesus Christ of Latter-day Saints in this dispensation (organized on April 6, 1830), the 175th anniversary of the first missionaries called in these latter days (in April 1830), the 170th anniversary of the calling of the Quorum of the Twelve Apostles (ordained in February 1835), and many other significant events.

Describing the momentous times in which we live, the Prophet Joseph Smith declared: "The building up of Zion is a cause that has interested the people of God in every age; it is a theme upon which prophets, priests and kings have dwelt with peculiar delight; they have looked forward with joyful anticipation to the day in which we live; and fired with heavenly and joyful anticipations they have sung and written and prophesied of this our day; *but they died without the sight; we are the favored people that God has made choice of to bring about the Latter-day glory.*"[6]

Notes

1. *Church History in the Fulness of Times,* Institute Student Manual, prepared by the Church Educational System (Salt Lake City: The Church of Jesus Christ of Latter-day Saints, 1989), 17.

2. Joseph Smith, *History of The Church of Jesus Christ of Latter-day Saints,* ed. B. H. Roberts, 2d ed. rev., 7 vols. (Salt Lake City: The Church of Jesus Christ of Latter-day Saints, 1980), 2:443.

3. Harold B. Lee, in Conference Reports of The Church of Jesus

Christ of Latter-day Saints (Salt Lake City: The Church of Jesus Christ of Latter-day Saints, 1898 to present), October 1947, 67.

4. Ibid., in Conference Reports, October 1973, 166.

5. Ibid., in Conference Reports, October 1947, 67.

6. Smith, *History of the Church,* 4:609–10.

CHAPTER ONE

THE RESTORATION
OF LIGHT AND TRUTH

RENEWAL OF LIGHT

Seventeenth-century artists employed a technique called *chiaroscuro* where the extreme contrasts between light and dark were used to achieve dramatic and emotional effect and to create depth. Because Rembrandt first painted his canvas backgrounds black, the contrasting lighter colors shimmered and stood out more. Similarly, the light of the restored gospel is all the more brilliant when painted across the darker landscape of the world. Thus, the Restoration is both a *declaration* of light as well as a *refutation* of darkness.

Given the challenges we face in today's world—when many "call evil good, and good evil; [and many mistake] darkness for light, and light for darkness" (Isaiah 5:20)—the absolute brilliance and blazing light of the restored gospel is all the more welcome. As Isaiah counseled us, "Arise, shine; for thy light is come, and the glory of the Lord is risen upon thee. For, behold, the darkness shall cover the earth, and gross darkness the people: but the Lord shall arise upon thee, and his glory shall be seen upon thee" (Isaiah 60:1–2). In 1833, the Lord declared to the Saints living in Kirtland, Ohio, that "the glory of God is intelligence, or, in other words, light and truth" (D&C 93:36). The message of the Restoration is that "intelligence" (or "light and truth") has been communicated from heaven once again.

During the month of December, we experience the

winter solstice—when the darkness of nighttime decreases and days begin to be filled with more light. It is no coincidence that we celebrate an important birth and commemorate another one during that time. Joseph Smith was born on December 23, and we celebrate the birth of Christ with the rest of the world on December 25. In the great premortal council, when the Father announced His plan for our happiness and eternal salvation and asked for a volunteer who would be willing to sacrifice himself in order to put the plan into effect and bless all others, it was Jesus who stepped forward and humbly but courageously answered: "Here am I, send me" (Abraham 3:27), "Father, thy will be done, and the glory be thine forever" (Moses 4:2). As Elder Neal A. Maxwell observed, "Never has anyone offered so much to so many in so few words!"[1] We sing a hymn containing the phrase, "Praise to the man who communed with Jehovah."[2] We praise Joseph Smith for helping us better understand how and why the Savior is our only hope of salvation—the Eternal Light of the world.

Spring—A Season of Renewal

When springtime arrives, a new day dawns and life is renewed. Even so, it was during the spring of 1820 when the First Vision occurred, and during the spring of 1830 when the Church of Jesus Christ was restored to the earth. When spring bursts upon the world, it happens almost overnight. Trees and flowers seem to come to life instantly and on cue. One week the weather is dark and uncertain, still in the clutches of cold and cloudy days, and the next week the sun breaks through the shadows so we can feel the warmth of its rays on our faces. So it was with the Restoration. One week the world was still gripped in general darkness and uncertainty, and the very next week, following the First Vision, the light of eternal life burst into view. A new day dawned for all mankind. Just as nature's springtime seems to fill our souls with anticipation for better days to come, the Restoration bears witness that our future is bright with possibility, with the hope and promise of eternal life for all.

The everlasting covenant, or the gospel of Jesus Christ, which was known in all previous gospel dispensations, has been sent into the world one last time as a *standard,* as a *light* for people to seek after, and as a *messenger* to prepare the way for the coming of the Lord (D&C 45:9). In 1838, the Savior declared to the members of the Church, "Verily I say unto you all, arise and shine forth, that thy light may be a standard for the nations" (D&C 115:5). Isaiah said the gospel would wave to all the world like an ensign, or banner, raised in the tops of the everlasting hills (Isaiah 5:26; 11:10, 12). And so it does. The Church, originally organized by Jesus Christ in the meridian of time, has been restored one final time to bless all mankind. A covenant community of Latter-day Saints has been established whose works and humanitarian efforts around the world reflect gospel light and radiate with the Spirit. The Savior declared that His followers would be recognized by their efforts to lift and bless others: "By their fruits ye shall know them" (Matthew 7:20). Thus, the events and unselfish acts of service with the Restoration stand as their own witness of the truth.

The Savior has also described His personal interest in saving mankind: "For behold, this is my work and my glory—to bring to pass the immortality and eternal life of man" (Moses 1:39). He has invited us to join Him in His work of saving souls and to do so without fear or worry: "For, behold, I am about to call upon [those in the world] to give heed to the light and glory of Zion, for the set time has come to favor her. Call ye, therefore, upon them with loud proclamation, and with your testimony, fearing them not, for they are as grass, and all their glory as the flower thereof which soon falleth, that they may be left also without excuse" (D&C 124:6–7).

The message of the Restoration is universal in its appeal, uniting in its message, exalting in the Spirit it carries, and will yet be preached to every nation and people (see Daniel 2:45; Revelation 14:6). But before the "kingdom of heaven may come" down from heaven to join us for the thousand-year millennium of peace, the kingdom of God must "go forth" across the earth (D&C 65:6). Therefore, the restored gospel of Jesus Christ must continue to roll across the entire earth until every heart and home has heard its message. It will eventually be even as Enoch described: "And righteousness will I send down out of heaven; and truth will I send forth out of the earth, to bear testimony of mine Only Begotten; his resurrection from the dead; yea, and also the resurrection of all men; and righteousness and truth will I cause to sweep the earth as with a flood, to gather out mine elect from the four quarters of the earth, unto a place which I shall prepare, an Holy City, that my people may gird up their loins, and be looking forth for the time of my coming; for there shall be my tabernacle, and it shall be called Zion, a New Jerusalem" (Moses 7:62).

The story of the Restoration, and the mounting evidences for its reality, will continue to spread across the earth like the rays of the rising of the sun. Our testimony is that the day of restoration has dawned and the brilliance of those restored rays bear witness of the Savior as the "light and life of the world." As prophesied, the restored Church of Jesus Christ is coming "out of the wilderness of darkness" and will "shine forth fair as the moon, clear as the sun" (D&C 109:73).

The Prophet Joseph was always willing to share his testimony of the Restoration with others. Elder Parley P. Pratt recorded an incident in Philadelphia where Joseph preached in a large church in January 1840:

> While visiting with brother Joseph in Philadelphia, a very large church was opened for him to preach in, and about three thousand people assembled to hear him. Brother Rigdon spoke first, and dwelt on the Gospel, illustrating his doctrine by the Bible. When he was through, brother Joseph arose like a lion about to roar; and being full of the Holy Ghost, spoke in great power, bearing testimony of the visions he had seen, the ministering of angels which he had enjoyed; and how he had found the plates of the Book of Mormon, and translated them by the gift and power of God. He commenced by saying: "If nobody else had the courage to testify of so glorious a message from Heaven, and of the finding of so glorious a record, he felt to do it in justice to the people, and leave the event with God."
>
> The entire congregation were astounded; electrified, as it were, and overwhelmed with the sense of the truth and power by which he spoke, and the wonders which he related. A lasting impression was made; many souls were gathered into the fold.[3]

Elder James E. Talmage once shared an experience he had as a student at Brigham Young University that taught him an important lesson about letting the gospel light shine in a positive way for others to see. As a student, he owned a small oil-burning study lamp. Because he depended upon it so much, he took excellent care of it, cleaning and trimming it daily. Elder Talmage related:

One summer evening I sat musing studiously and withal restfully in the open air outside the door of the room in which I lodged and studied. A stranger approached. I noticed that he carried a satchel. He was affable and entertaining. I brought another chair from within, and we chatted together till the twilight had deepened into darkness.

Then he said, "You are a student, and doubtless have much work to do o'nights. What kind of lamp do you use?" And without waiting for a reply he continued: "I have a superior lamp I should like to show you, a lamp designed and constructed according to the latest achievements of science, far surpassing anything heretofore produced as a means of artificial lighting."

I replied with confidence, and I confess not without some exultation: "My friend, I have a lamp, one that has been tested and proved. It has been to me a companion through many a long night. It is an Argand lamp, and one of the best. I have trimmed and cleaned it today; it is ready for the lighting. Step inside; I will show you my lamp, then you may tell me whether yours can possibly be better."

We entered my study room, and with a feeling that I assume is akin to that of the athlete about to enter a contest with one whom he regards as a pitiably inferior opponent, I put the match to my well-trimmed Argand.

My visitor was voluble in his praise. It was the best lamp of its kind he said. He averred that he had never seen a lamp in better trim. He turned the wick up and down and pronounced the adjustment perfect. He declared that never before had he realized how satisfactory a student lamp could be.

I liked the man; he seemed to me wise, and he assuredly was ingratiating. . . .

"Now," said he, "with your permission I'll light *my* lamp." He took from his satchel a lamp then known as the "Rochester." It had a chimney which, compared with mine, was as a factory smoke-stack alongside a house flue. Its hollow wick was wide enough to admit my four fingers. Its light made bright the remotest corner of my room. In its brilliant blaze my own little Argand wick burned a weak, pale yellow. Until that moment of convincing demonstration I had never known the dim obscurity in which I had lived and labored, studied and struggled.

"I'll buy your lamp," said I; "you need neither explain nor argue further." I took my new acquisition to the laboratory that same night, and determined its capacity. It turned at over forty-eight candle power—fully four times the intensity of my student lamp.

Two days after purchasing, I met the lamp-peddler on the street, about noontime. To my inquiry he replied that business was good; the demand for his lamps was greater than the factory supply. "But," said I, "you are not working today?" His rejoinder was a lesson: "Do you think that I would be so foolish as to go around trying to sell lamps in the daytime? Would you have bought one if I had lighted it for you when the sun was shining? I chose the time to show the superiority of my lamp over yours; and you were eager to own the better one I offered, were you not?"

Such is the story. Now consider the application of a part, a very small part, thereof.

"Let your light so shine before men, that they may see your good works, and glorify your Father, which is in heaven."

The man who would sell me a lamp did not disparage mine. He placed his greater light along side my feebler flame, and I hastened to obtain the better.

The [members] of the Church of Jesus Christ today are sent forth, not to assail nor ridicule the beliefs of men, but to set before the world a superior light, by which the smoky dimness of the flickering flames of man-made [beliefs] shall be apparent. The work of the Church is constructive, not destructive.[4]

As Elder Talmage's parable illustrates, Latter-day Saints have the responsibility to hold up the light of the Restoration for others to see. President John Taylor commented: "We must not forget that we owe a duty to the world. The Lord has given to us the light of eternity; and we are commanded not to conceal our light under a bushel. . . . We want men [and women] full of the Holy Ghost and the power of God that they may go forth . . . bearing precious seed and sowing the seeds of eternal life, and then returning with gladness, bringing their sheaves with them."[5]

The gospel of Jesus Christ is the most positive force on the earth for good. Regardless, however, of how bright the light of the Restoration may shine, the "mists of darkness [which] are the temptations of the devil" (1 Nephi 12:17) can blind eyes, harden hearts, and lead people away from the things that really matter most. In one of the last speeches President Brigham Young gave, he wisely warned, "Many professing to be saints seem to have no knowledge, no light, to see anything beyond a dollar, or a pleasant time, a comfortable house, a fine farm & C. These have their place, but what do we enjoy? 'O fools, and slow of heart to understand the purposes of God and his handiwork among his people.'"[6]

Prophets have reminded us that the time has come when we can no longer stand as witnesses of the Restoration using borrowed light, but that every person has the privilege and obligation to receive their own witness of the truth. President Joseph F. Smith said:

> One fault to be avoided by the Saints, young and old, is the tendency to live on *borrowed light,* with their own hidden under a bushel; to permit the savor of their salt of knowledge to be lost; and the light within them to be reflected, rather than original. . . .
>
> Men and women should become settled in the truth, and *founded in the knowledge of the gospel,* depending upon no person for borrowed or reflected light, but trusting only upon the Holy Spirit, who is ever the same, shining forever and testifying to the individual and the priesthood, who live in harmony with the laws of the gospel, of the glory and the will of the Father. They will then have light everlasting which cannot be obscured. By its shining in their lives, they shall cause others to glorify God; and by their well-doing put to silence the ignorance of foolish men, and show forth the praises of him who hath called them out of darkness into his marvelous light.[7]

THAT WE MIGHT HAVE ETERNAL LIFE

The Savior declared to those He served in His own lifetime: "I am come that they might have life, and that they might have it more abundantly" (John 10:10). A short time later, when He appeared as a resurrected being to the Nephites and Lamanites living in ancient America, the risen Lord affirmed: "Yea, verily I say unto you, if ye will come unto me ye shall have eternal life. Behold, mine arm of mercy is extended towards you, and whosoever will come, him will I receive; and blessed are those who come unto me" (3 Nephi 9:14). In our own time, He has declared, "Learn that he who doeth the works of righteousness shall receive his reward, even peace in this world, and eternal life in the world to come" (D&C 59:23). To all the world, the Eternal Father has declared, "I am God, and have sent mine Only Begotten Son into the world for the redemption of the world, and have decreed that he that receiveth him shall be saved, and he that receiveth him not shall be damned" (D&C 49:5).

To help us receive these promised blessings, the Father and the Son have appeared once again in our day, called living prophets, given them words to speak, and commanded them to go forth and teach. "What I the Lord have spoken, I have spoken," He has revealed, "and I excuse not myself; and though the heavens and the earth pass away, my word shall not pass away, but shall all be fulfilled, *whether by mine own voice or by the voice of my servants, it is the same*" (D&C 1:38; emphasis added). Prophets just like Adam and Abraham, Moses and Melchizedek are once again found on earth. Apostles just like Peter, James, John the Revelator, and Paul preside over the restored Church of Jesus Christ in these last days. The Prophet called of God to succeed all previous prophets was the Prophet Joseph Smith, and his successors continue to hold all the keys, rights, powers and authority given him by God and angels. The work he commenced will continue until it accomplishes all God intends it to. Truly did Joseph Smith prophesy: "The Standard of Truth has been erected; no unhallowed hand can stop the work from progressing; persecutions may rage, mobs may combine, armies may assemble, calumny may defame, but the truth of God will go forth boldly, nobly, and independent, till it has penetrated every continent, visited every clime, swept every country, and sounded in every ear, till the purposes of God shall be accomplished, and the Great Jehovah shall say the work is done."[8]

We are committed to the work of the Restoration because it is the Lord's work, as revealed by Him. As the First Presidency testified in 1907: "Our motives are not selfish; our purposes not petty and earth-bound; we contemplate the human race, past, present and yet to come, as immortal beings, for whose salvation it is our mission to labor: and to this work, broad as eternity and deep as the love of God, we devote ourselves, now, and forever."[9]

Brigham Young, perhaps, said it best: "I feel like shouting hallelujah, all the time, when I think that I ever knew Joseph Smith, the Prophet whom the Lord raised up and ordained, and to whom He gave keys and power to build up the kingdom of God on earth and sustain it. These keys are committed to this people, and we have power to continue the work that Joseph commenced, until everything is prepared for the coming of the Son of Man. This is the business of the Latter-day Saints, and it is all the business we have on hand."[10]

The Restoration is an open invitation to all mankind to come and receive more light and truth than presently available. The Prophet Joseph declared: "I have no desire but to do all men good. . . . *We don't ask any people to throw away any good they have got; we only ask them to come and get more.* What if all the world should embrace this Gospel? They would then see eye to eye, and the blessings of God would be poured out upon the people, which is the desire of my whole soul."[11] The *gospel* is the *good news* of Jesus Christ, and, as Joseph Smith noted, "The word *Mormon,* means literally, *more good.*"[12]

Notes

1. Neal A. Maxwell, *Even As I Am* (Salt Lake City: Deseret Book, 1982), 115.

2. *Hymns of The Church of Jesus Christ of Latter-day Saints* (Salt Lake City: The Church of Jesus Christ of Latter-day Saints, 1985), no. 27.

3. Parley P. Pratt, *The Autobiography of Parley P. Pratt,* ed. Parley P. Pratt Jr. (Salt Lake City: Deseret Book, 1985), 260.

4. *The Parables of Elder James E. Talmage,* comp. Albert L. Zobell Jr. (Salt Lake City: Deseret Book, 1973), 3–6.

5. John Taylor, in *Journal of Discourses,* 26 vols. (London: Latter-day Saints' Book Depot, 1854–86), 21:375.

6. Brigham Young, in *Journal of Discourses,* 8:63.

7. Joseph F. Smith, *Gospel Doctrine,* 19th ed. (Salt Lake City: Deseret Book, 1978), 87–88; emphasis added.

8. Joseph Smith, *History of The Church of Jesus Christ of Latter-day Saints,* ed. B. H. Roberts, 2d ed. rev., 7 vols. (Salt Lake City: The Church of Jesus Christ of Latter-day Saints, 1980), 4:540.

9. Joseph F. Smith, John R. Winder, and Anthon H. Lund, "Message of the First Presidency," in Conference Reports of The Church of Jesus Christ of Latter-day Saints (Salt Lake City: The Church of Jesus Christ of Latter-day Saints, 1898 to present), April 1907, Appendix, 16.

10. Young, in *Journal of Discourses,* 3:51.

11. Smith, *History of the Church,* 5:259.

12. Smith, *History of the Church,* 5:400.

CHAPTER TWO

"A MARVELOUS WORK AND A WONDER"

Mosiah Hancock recalled an experience he had as a young boy with the Prophet Joseph Smith in Nauvoo: "[In] the summer of 1841 I played my first game of ball with the Prophet. We took turns knocking and chasing the ball. And when the game was over . . . he told them to cut wood for the Saints who needed it."[1] Was it any wonder that they loved that great, good man?

Reflecting on the Prophet's death just four years later in 1844, Mosiah recorded:

> I saw the prophet and the rest when they departed from Nauvoo for the last time; and I went out to meet their martyred bodies when they were brought from Carthage. . . .
>
> I went to see those noble martyrs after they were laid out in the mansion. . . . [A] great stream of people continued until the saints all had the privilege of taking their last look at the martyred bodies.
>
> After the people had gone home, my father took me again into the mansion and told me to place one hand on Joseph's breast and to raise my other arm and swear, with hand uplifted, that I would never make a compromise with any of the sons of Hell. Which vow I took with a determination to fulfill to the very letter. I took the same vow with Hyrum.[2]

Can you imagine the impact such an experience would have on a young man? Studying the great events associated with the history of the restored church and the life and teachings of the Prophet Joseph Smith can have a similar impact on us. As we hold the scriptures of the Restoration or the writings of the modern prophets in our hands, it can be as if, spiritually speaking, we are placing our hands over their hearts. As we read, we can renew the determination in our hearts to "never make a compromise" with the wickedness of this world. There is spiritual power to be found in studying the scriptures and doctrines of the Restoration.

STRENGTH OF THE MORMON POSITION

If Joseph Smith had claimed that he was Jesus Christ returned to the earth or had taught that there was no need to believe in Jesus Christ as our Lord and Redeemer, then the animosity and persecution that resulted in his death might be comprehensible. But he did not. In fact, Joseph Smith was one of the most powerful testifiers of the resurrected Lord and Savior Jesus Christ the world has ever known.

The strength of his testimony is that it was based on revelation. Elder Orson F. Whitney noted that "'Mormonism' means far more than the restoration of the Gospel at the beginning of the Nineteenth Century. . . . 'Mormonism' is not a mere sect among sects, one more broken off fragment of a degenerate and crumbling Christianity. It is the pure, primitive Christianity restored—the original faith, the root of all religion; and it was not accident, but design, that gave it the strength of its position."[3]

As President Gordon B. Hinckley has testified, the validity of the work we are engaged in rests on the cornerstone of the First Vision: "Our whole strength rests on the validity of that vision. It either occurred or it did not occur.

If it did not, then this work is a fraud. If it did, then it is the most important and wonderful work under the heavens."[4]

President George Q. Cannon similarly commented, "If it were not for the new revelations received from the Almighty, this people called Latter-day Saints would not be in existence. If it were not that the Lord has revealed in great plainness his mind and will unto his people, they would not be an organization, neither would his Elders have gone forth bearing testimony of the truths of the everlasting Gospel."[5] Without the revelations and priesthood keys and authority given to the Prophet Joseph Smith, The Church of Jesus Christ of Latter-day Saints would not exist.

Never Claimed Preeminence

Joseph Smith never claimed to be perfect, nor did he feel he was better than other people. He simply testified of his call from God and proclaimed the gospel of Jesus Christ as it was revealed to him. Joseph recognized that although called of God, he was like other men and women. He recognized that he was not perfect but continued to testify that the work he was doing was inspired and from God: "Although I was called of my Heavenly Father to lay the foundation of this great work and kingdom in this dispensation, and testify of His revealed will to scattered Israel, I am subject to like passions as other men, like the prophets of olden times."[6] Joseph humbly acknowledged his own weakness and pledged to stand by others despite their weaknesses: "I told them I was but a man, and they must not expect me to be perfect; if they expected perfection from me, I should expect it from them; but if they would bear with my infirmities and the infirmities of the brethren, I would likewise bear with their infirmities."[7] True enough, he was "but a man," but he was empowered with a divine mission and calling from

God. Elder James E. Faust has said, "As I submit to you my testimony of Joseph Smith, I acknowledge his humanness along with his great spiritual powers. He did not claim to be divine, nor a perfect man. He claimed only to be a mortal man with human feelings and imperfections, trying honestly to fulfill the divine mission given to him."[8]

It is important to remember what the Prophet Joseph said of himself and of the revelations he received: "I never told you I was perfect; but there is no error in the revelations which I have taught."[9] Dennison L. Harris reported hearing Joseph Smith's own testimony about the Restoration: "I am no false prophet; I am no impostor. I have had no dark revelations, I have had no revelations from the devil. I have made no revelations; I have not got anything up myself."[10] He knew what he was to do because he had been not only called but tutored of God: "I know what I say; I understand my mission and business."[11] Later he added, "I have got all the truth which the Christian world possessed, and an independent revelation in the bargain, and God will bear me off triumphant."[12]

Joseph received his first counsel from God the Father: "This is my beloved Son. Hear him!" (Joseph Smith–History 1:17). Joseph Smith listened carefully to Jesus then and ever after.

NOTHING SHORT OF MIRACULOUS

The story of the Restoration is real, yet so incredible that near the end of his life, the Prophet Joseph Smith exclaimed to an audience in Nauvoo, "I don't blame anyone for not believing my history. If I had not experienced what I have, I could not have believed it myself."[13]

The First Vision of the Prophet Joseph Smith initiated a glorious time of restitution. It is astonishing to contemplate what the Lord accomplished through the Prophet Joseph Smith during his very short life. It is astounding and nothing short of miraculous—truly the Restoration is "a marvelous work and a wonder," just as the Lord described it would be (2 Nephi 25:17; 27:26; Isaiah 29:14). Even in our own day, miracles continue to be poured out upon this work.

The work of the Restoration is indeed "marvelous" and will yet be seen as a "wonder"—a wonderful blessing to all who will receive it. God has said, "I [will] bring to pass my strange act" (D&C 95:4; 101:95) and He has commanded us to bring to the world things "they have never considered" (D&C 101:94). The world, in fact, will marvel and wonder at what will be accomplished, but as the Savior declared, the miracles attending the Restoration and the growth of the Restored Church should not come as any surprise: "Therefore, marvel not at these things, for ye are not yet pure; ye can not yet bear my glory; but ye shall behold it if ye are faithful in keeping all my words that I have given you, from the days of Adam to Abraham, from Abraham to Moses, from Moses to Jesus and his apostles, and from Jesus and his apostles to Joseph Smith, whom I did call upon by mine angels, my ministering servants, and by mine own voice out of the heavens, to bring forth my work" (D&C 136:37).

MODERN MIRACLES PARALLEL CHURCH GROWTH

We live in the promised day when God said He would pour out His spirit "upon all flesh," when many young men and young women would "dream dreams" and "see visions" (Joel 2:28), when "knowledge shall be increased" and poured out almost without measure, when we would be "ever learning" (Daniel 12:4; 2 Timothy 3:7). Isaiah foresaw our day as a time when the Lord's work would be hastened by the ability to travel swiftly across the earth (Isaiah 18:1–3; 2 Nephi 15:26–27). With the help of modern telecommunications and technology, the day quickly approaches when "the earth shall be full of the knowledge of the Lord, as the waters cover the sea" (Isaiah 11:9).

It is interesting to note that from the days of Adam and Eve until the time of the Restoration, the quickest anyone could travel or communicate was by horse or horse-drawn carriages. Susa Young Gates "once asked her father, President Brigham Young, how it would ever be possible to accomplish the great amount of temple work that must be done. . . . He told her there would be many inventions of labor-saving devices, so that our daily duties could be performed in a short time, leaving us more and more time for temple work. The inventions have come, and are still coming."[14]

The moment the gospel was restored to the earth, modern inventions in transportation and communication began to be developed—and have paralleled the growth of the Church.[15] This is not merely a coincidence but divine design. Until the gospel was restored in 1830, travel and communication was limited across the entire earth. Every modern form of transportation and telecommunication was revealed following the Restoration, and there is great meaning to this. All the marvelous inventions and modern conveniences we enjoy enable the gospel, in one way or another, to be taken to more people than ever before. Thus, more individuals and nations can know the truth in our modern era than in all previous eras of world history combined.

Appreciation begins with recognition. Recognizing the hand of the Lord in His latter-day work enriches our ability to appreciate and show gratitude for the marvelous work and wonder of the Restoration. But, to understand the need for the Restoration, we first need to understand what happened in the Great Apostasy that preceded it.

➤ ◄

The Great Apostasy—
Loss of Light and Truth

Despite persecution, the Church of Jesus Christ flourished in the apostolic era. "But as the centuries passed, the flame flickered and dimmed. Ordinances were changed or abandoned. The line was broken, and the authority to confer the Holy Ghost as a gift was gone. The Dark Ages of apostasy settled over the world."[16] Thus, following the days of Jesus and the apostles, "the Church, as an earthly organization operating under divine direction and having authority to officiate in spiritual ordinances, ceased to exist."[17] The New Testament record makes it clear that Peter was given the keys of the kingdom and was called to lead the early Church after the death of Jesus Christ (Matthew 16:19). Tradition holds that Peter was arrested in Rome and crucified during the reign of Nero (the Roman leader who mercilessly persecuted Christians and blamed them for the burning of Rome in A.D. 64). One by one the original apostles called by Jesus were similarly slain until those who held the keys of the kingdom were gone. "Wherefore, the tares choke[d] the wheat and [drove] the church into the wilderness" (D&C 86:3).

Many in modern Christianity deny that a universal apostasy from the early Church ever occurred.[18] Yet, "the church founded by Jesus and the apostles did not survive and was not expected to. . . . Jesus himself insisted that the light was to be taken away. . . . [He] announced in no uncertain terms that his message would be rejected by all men, as the message of the prophets had been before,[19] and that he would soon leave the world to die in its sins and seek after him in vain."[20, 21]

The Greek word *apostasía*, from which we derived the English word *apostasy*, "is constructed from two Greek roots: the verb *hist'mi*, 'to stand,' and the preposition *apϛ*, 'away from.' The word means 'rebellion,' 'mutiny,' 'revolt,' or 'revolution,' and it is used in ancient contexts with reference to uprisings against established authority."[22] False teachers and unfaithful members rebelled against Church authority. Evidence for the Apostasy is found in the New Testament itself. The writings of the ancient apostles, including those of John, predicted this mutinous falling away[23] and declared that it was already upon them.[24] The fact that the Lord described His restored gospel as having come "out of obscurity and out of darkness" indicates how complete the darkness of apostasy was (D&C 1:30). But the scriptures also foretold of a future restoration, an event to occur in the latter days.[25]

This apostasy began during the days of the apostles and was referred to frequently in their writings.[26] As a result of the Apostasy, it became necessary to again restore and reorganize the Church of Jesus Christ on the earth in the latter days (D&C 86:1–4).

APOSTASY IN EACH DISPENSATION NECESSITATES A RESTORATION

The Great Apostasy that occurred after the apostles were removed from the earth was not the first apostasy to occur. No sooner had the gospel been established in the beginning with Adam and Eve than apostasy began to encroach upon the truth. Apostasy from the true Church occurred as the children of Adam and Eve forsook the revealed principles and ordinances of the gospel of Jesus Christ: "Adam and Eve blessed the name of God and they made all things known unto their sons and their daughters [but] Satan came among them . . . and he commanded them, saying: Believe it not; and they believed it not, and they loved Satan more than

God. And men began from that time forth to be carnal, sensual, and devilish" (Moses 5:12–13).

Throughout human history, whenever such an apostasy occurred, the gospel and the saving ordinances were *revealed* or *dispensed* from heaven anew, according to the divine pattern. There have been many gospel dispensations since the beginning. A "*dispensation* of the gospel is a period of time in which the Lord has at least one authorized servant on the earth who bears the holy priesthood and the keys, and who has a divine commission to *dispense* the gospel to the inhabitants of the earth."[27] The scriptures identify several gospel dispensations following the days of Adam, including in the days of Enoch, Noah, Abraham, Moses, and even Jesus Christ. Thus, the Church organized in the meridian of time by the Lord Jesus Christ and His apostolic ministers was also a restored Church, revealed according to the divine pattern (Matthew 16:13–19).

The fact that there has been a restoration is the best evidence that an apostasy from the Church established by Jesus Christ in the meridian of time occurred (D&C 1:14–17, 30). Following the divine pattern—customary in every former dispensation—the Holy Ghost inspired worthy souls and the Lord revealed His Church once again with all its saving ordinances to living prophets and apostles. The chosen servant through whom the Restoration in this final dispensation would be accomplished was Joseph Smith (D&C 5:10). In December 1830, the Lord reiterated in a revelation that He was sending the fullness of His restored gospel "by the hand of my servant Joseph" (D&C 35:17).

God can only be known by revelation. He either reveals Himself or remains forever unknown (Jacob 4:8). When revelation ceases, so does the true knowledge of God—what He is like, who He is, and how we can become like Him. Joseph Smith's message to the world is that God has spoken to mankind once again and revealed Himself that we might know Him.

Notes

1. Transcribed from "Impressions of a Prophet," the Carthage Jail Visitors Center video presentation. In his journal, Mosiah Hancock observed, "Everybody loved to do as the Prophet said. . . . The people loved him" (*Encyclopedia of Joseph Smith's Teachings,* ed. Larry E. Dahl and Donald Q. Cannon (Salt Lake City: Deseret Book, 1997), 107–8.

2. Mosiah Lyman Hancock, *The Life Story of Mosiah Lyman Hancock* (Provo, Utah: Brigham Young University, 1956), 20.

3. Orson F. Whitney, *Strength of the "Mormon" Position* (Salt Lake City: Deseret News Press, 1917), 27–28.

4. Gordon B. Hinckley, "The Marvelous Foundation of Our Faith," *Ensign,* November 2002, 80.

5. George Q. Cannon, in *Journal of Discourses,* 26 vols. (London: Latter-day Saints' Book Depot, 1854–86), 19:104.

6. Joseph Smith, *History of the Church of Jesus Christ of Latter-day Saints,* ed. B. H. Roberts, 2d ed. rev., 7 vols. (Salt Lake City: The Church of Jesus Christ of Latter-day Saints, 1980), 5:516.

7. Ibid., 5:181.

8. James E. Faust, in Conference Reports of The Church of Jesus Christ of Latter-day Saints (Salt Lake City: The Church of Jesus Christ of Latter-day Saints, 1898 to present), October 1981, 106.

9. Joseph Smith, *Teachings of the Prophet Joseph Smith,* comp. Joseph Fielding Smith (Salt Lake City: Deseret Book, 1976), 368.

10. Dennison L. Harris, statement to President Joseph F. Smith, Ephraim, Utah, 15 May 1881, recorded by George F. Gibbs, LDS Church Archives, Salt Lake City, as cited in Horace Cummings, "Conspiracy of Nauvoo," *The Contributor* (April 1884): 259.

11. Smith, *History of the Church,* 5:259.

12. Ibid., 6:479.

13. Ibid., 6:317.

14. Archibald F. Bennett, "Put On Thy Strength, O Zion!" *Improvement Era* (October 1952): 720.

15. Joseph Fielding Smith, in Conference Reports, October 1926, 117; Howard W. Hunter, "We Have a Work to Do," *Ensign,*

March 1995, 65; Bennett, "Put On Thy Strength, O Zion!" 720.

16. Boyd K. Packer, "The Cloven Tongues of Fire," *Ensign,* May 2000, 8.

17. Ezra Taft Benson, in Conference Reports, October 1949, 26; see also Acts 20:29; 2 Thessalonians 2:3; Galatians 1:6–8; 2 Peter 2:1.

18. Some notable exceptions of Christian writers who agree that significant changes occurred and that modern Christianity no longer resembles the early Church include David W. Bercot, *Will the Real Heretics Please Stand Up?* (Tyler, Texas: Scroll Publishing, 1989); and Mark A. Noll, *Turning Points—Decisive Moments in the History of Christianity* (Leicester, England: Baker Books, 1997).

19. References cited here by Dr. Hugh W. Nibley: Matthew 17:12; 21:37–39; 23:31–37; Mark 12:6–8; Luke 17:25; John 1:5, 10–11; 3:11–12, 19, 32; 5:38, 40–47; 7:7; 8:19, 23–24, 37–38, 40–47; 15:22–25; cf. Acts 3:13–15 ("The Passing of the Primitive Church," in *When the Lights Went Out—Three Studies on the Ancient Apostasy* (Provo, Utah: FARMS, 2001), 29n6.

20. References cited here by Dr. Hugh W. Nibley: Matthew 9:15; Luke 9:41; 13:25–27; 17:22; John 12:33–36; 13:33; 14:30; 16:16; cf. Acts 3:21 ("The Passing of the Primitive Church," in *When the Lights Went Out,* 29n7).

21. Nibley, "The Passing of the Primitive Church," 2–3.

22. Kent P. Jackson, *From Apostasy to Restoration* (Salt Lake City: Deseret Book, 1996), 9.

23. Acts 20:29; 2 Timothy 4:4; 1 John 2:18–19.

24. 1 Timothy 1:6; John 6:66; 1 John 2:18; 1 John 4:1.

25. Matthew 17:11; 24:14; Acts 3:21; Revelation 14:6.

26. Matthew 24:4–14; Acts 20:28–30; 2 Timothy 3:1–5, 13; 4:3–4.

27. LDS Bible Dictionary, s.v. "Dispensations," 657; emphasis added.

CHAPTER THREE

PERSONALITY OF THE PROPHET

In addition to his divine calling, Joseph Smith also had a compelling personal charisma that endeared him to many people—including even some of his enemies.

Elder Parley P. Pratt, who spent much time with the Prophet Joseph, observed, "His manner was easy and familiar;. . . . He interested and edified while, at the same time, he amused and entertained his audience; and none listened to him that were ever weary with his discourse. I have even known him to retain a congregation of willing and anxious listeners for many hours together, in the midst of cold or sunshine, rain or wind, while they were laughing at one moment and weeping the next. Even his most bitter enemies were generally overcome, if he could once get their ears."[1]

An incident at Far West, Missouri (headquarters of the Church in 1838), illustrates just such a moment. Joseph Smith was at his parents' home writing a letter. The Prophet's mother recorded what happened:

> Eight [members of the state militia] came into the house. Thinking they had come for some refreshment, I offered them chairs. . . .
> "We do not choose to sit down, we have come here to kill Joe Smith and all the Mormons."
> "Ah," said I, "What has Joseph Smith done, that you should want to kill him?"
> "He has killed seven men in Davies County," replied the foremost, "and we have

come to kill him and all his Church."

"He has not been in Daviess county," I answered, "consequently, the report must be false. Furthermore, if you should see him you would not want to kill him."

"There is no doubt that the report is perfectly correct," rejoined the officer; "it came straight to us, and I believe it; and we were sent to kill the Prophet and all who believe in him, and I'll be d—-d if I don't execute my orders."

"I suppose," said I, "you intend to kill me, with the rest?"

"Yes, we do," returned the officer.

"Very well," I continued, "I want you to act the gentleman about it, and do the job quick. Just shoot me down at once, then I shall be at rest; but I should not like to be murdered by inches."

"There it is again," said he. "You tell a 'Mormon' that you will kill him, and they will always tell you, 'that is nothing—if you kill us, we shall be happy.'"

Joseph, just at this moment finished his letter, and, seeing that he was at liberty, I said, "Gentlemen, suffer me to make you acquainted with Joseph Smith, the Prophet." They stared at him as if he were a spectre. He smiled, and stepping towards them, gave each of them his hand, in a manner which convinced them that he was neither a guilty criminal nor yet a hypocrite.

Joseph then sat down and explained to them the views & feelings, etc., of the Church, and what their course had been; besides the treatment which they had received from their enemies since the first. He also argued, that if any one of the brethren had broken the law, they ought to be tried by the law, before anyone else was molested. After talking with them some time in this way, he said, "Mother, I believe I will go home now—Emma will be expecting me."

At this two of the men sprang to their feet, and declared that he should not go alone, as it would be unsafe—that they would go with him, in order to protect him. Accordingly the three left together, and, during their absence, I overheard the following conversation among the officers, who remained at the door:

1st Officer. "Did you not feel strangely when Smith took you by the hand? I never felt so in my life."

2nd Officer. "I could not move. I would not harm a hair of that man's head for the whole world."

3rd Officer. "This is the last time you will catch me coming to kill Joe Smith, or the 'Mormons' either."

1st Officer. "I guess this is about my last expedition against this place. I never saw a more harmless, innocent appearing man than the 'Mormon' Prophet."

2nd Officer. "That story about his killing them men is all a d—d lie—there is no doubt of it; and we have had all this trouble for nothing; but they will never fool me in this way again; I'll warrant them."[2]

Joseph Smith's personality had the same effect on the Saints. After his death, his wife Emma wrote a letter to one of their sons and said,

I do not expect you can do much more in the garden than your father could, and I never wanted him to go out into the garden to work for if he did it would not be fifteen minutes before there would be three or four or sometimes a half dozen men around him and they would tramp the ground down faster than he could hoe it up.[3]

"Lorenzo Snow and Parley P. Pratt felt that 'there never was a man who possessed a higher degree of integrity that Joseph Smith.'[4] Jesse W. Crosby observed that Joseph Smith had an 'unfailing habit' of always sharpening an ax before returning it to the person he had borrowed it from, and if he borrowed a sack of flour from somebody he always repaid the debt with more flour than he had first received. His philosophy was that 'anything borrowed should be returned always with interest to the lender.'"[5]

Joseph possessed a positive attitude and had a "native cheery temperament" that naturally attracted people to him (Joseph Smith–History 1:28). Benjamin F. Johnson said that he and others took "great delight in his [Joseph's] society and friendship." He added, "When with us, there was no lack of amusement; for with jokes, games, etc., he was always ready to provoke merriment, one phase of which was matching couplets in rhyme, by which we were at times in rivalry; and his fraternal feeling, in great degree did away with the disparity of age or greatness of his calling."[6]

We might expect devoted followers to honor him with tributes. But there are many neutral observers who were also impressed with Joseph Smith. One of these was Josiah Quincy, a Boston mayor who met the Prophet Joseph. In a speech before the Philadelphia Historical Society in 1883, he said:

It is by no means improbable that some
future text-book, for the use of generations yet
unborn will contain a question like this: "What
historical American of the nineteenth century
has exerted the most powerful influence upon
the destinies of his countrymen?" And it is
by no means improbable that the answer to
that interrogatory may thus be written: Joseph
Smith the Mormon Prophet.[7]

Judge Stephen A. Douglas, who ran as a candidate for
U.S. president, was impressed with Joseph Smith's leadership and said, "If I could command the following of Joseph
Smith, I would resign my seat in Congress and go to
Oregon. In five years a noble state might be formed, and if
they wouldn't receive us into the Union, we would have a
government of our own."[8]

A historian named Samuel Smucker wrote: "It cannot be
denied that [Joseph Smith] was one of the most extraordinary persons of his time, a man of rude genius, who accomplished a much greater work than he knew; and whose name,
whatever he may have been whilst living, will take its place
among the notabilities of the world."[9]

Even the *New York Sun*, on September 4, 1843 (just a few
months before the Prophet was slain), published this statement: "This Joe Smith must be an extraordinary character.
He is one of the great men of this age, and in future history
he will be ranked with those who in one way or another have
stamped their impress strongly on society."[10]

One reason for his influence on people was the love
and compassion he showed them. On one occasion he said,
"Sectarian priests cry out concerning me, and ask, 'Why is
it this babbler gains so many followers, and retains them?' I
answer, It is because I possess the principle of love. All I can

offer the world is a good heart and a good hand."[11] Joseph Smith commented, "I freely forgive all men. If we would secure and cultivate the love of others, we must love others, even our enemies as well as friends."[12] He also taught, "To be justified before God we must love one another: we must overcome evil; we must visit the fatherless and the widow in their affliction, and we must keep ourselves unspotted from the world: for such virtues flow from the great fountain of pure religion."[13] In his final address to the Saints, he said, "I never did harm any man since I was born in the world. My voice is always for peace. . . . I never think any evil, nor do anything to the harm of my fellowman."[14]

Illustrative of one of the hundreds of kind deeds Joseph Smith did for others is an incident involving John E. Page. Elder Page was called on a mission to Canada but delayed leaving Kirtland because he was destitute of warm clothing. President Thomas S. Monson described what happened in these words:

> We demonstrate our love by how well we serve our God. Remember when the Prophet Joseph Smith went to John E. Page and said to him, "Brother Page, you have been called on a mission to Canada."
>
> Brother Page, struggling for an excuse, said, "Brother Joseph, I can't go to Canada. I don't have a coat to wear."
>
> The Prophet took off his own coat, handed it to John Page, and said, "Wear this, and the Lord will bless you."
>
> John Page went on his mission to Canada. In two years he walked something like 5,000 miles and baptized 600 converts. (See Andrew Jenson, "John E. Page," *The Historical Record,* 5:572.) He was successful

because he responded to an opportunity to serve his God.[15]

Joseph and Emma Smith's kindnesses to others won the hearts of many. Jane Manning James, a freeborn black woman from Connecticut, walked a thousand miles with her extended family to Nauvoo, Illinois, in 1843 to join the Saints. She described her experience meeting Joseph and Emma and being the recipient of their benevolence:

> Yes, indeed, I guess I did know the Prophet Joseph. That lovely hand! He used to put it out to me. Never passed me without shaking hands with me wherever he was. Oh, he was the finest man I ever saw on earth.
> . . . I . . . think about Brother Joseph and Sister Emma and how good they was to me. When I went there [to Nauvoo] I only had two things on me, no shoes nor stockings, wore them all out on the road. I had a trunk full of beautiful clothes, which I had sent around by water, and I was thinking of having them when I got to Nauvoo, and they stole them at St. Louis, and I did not have a rag of them.
> . . . Sister Emma she come to the door first and she says, "Walk in, come in all of you," and she went up stairs, and down he comes and goes into the sitting room and told the girls that they had there, he wanted to have the room this evening, for we have got company come. I knew it was Brother Joseph because I had seen him in a dream. He went and brought Dr. Bernhisel down and Sister Emma, and introduced him to everyone of us, and said, "Now, I want you to tell me about some of your hard trials. I want to hear of

some of those hard trials." And we told him. He slapped his hands.

"Dr. Bernhisel," he said, "what do you think of that?" And he said,

"I think if I had had it to do I should not have come; would not have had faith enough."

[The family stayed with the Smith's for a week until they were all settled in places to stay.]

He [Joseph Smith] came in every morning to see us and shake hands and know how we all were. One morning, before he came in, I had been up to the landing and found all my clothes were gone. Well, I sat there crying. He came in and looked around.

"Why where's all the folks?"

"Why brother," I says, "they have all got themselves places; but," I says, "I haint got any place," and I burst out a-crying.

"We won't have tears here," he says.

"But," I says, "I have got no home."

"Well you've got a home here," he says, "Have you seen Sister Emma this morning?"

"No, sir," I says.

So he started out and went upstairs and brought Sister Emma down and says, "Here's a girl who says she's got no home. Don't you think she's got a home here?"

And she says, "If she wants to stay here."

And he says, "Do you want to stay here?"

"Yes, sir," says I. "Well, now," he says, "Sister Emma you just talk to her and see how she is." He says, "Good morning," and he went.

. . . I did not talk much to him, but every

time he saw me he would say, "God bless you," and pat me on the shoulder. To Sister Emma, he said, "go and clothe her up, go down to the store and clothe her up." Sister Emma did. She got me clothes by the bolt. I had everything.[16]

Jane Snyder Richards recorded what it was like for new converts to meet the Prophet and be greeted by him for the first time: "I first saw the Prophet Joseph Smith and shook hands with him, in a dream, about eighteen months before my removal to Nauvoo. Later, at Nauvoo, from the recollections of my dream, I recognized him at first sight, while he was preaching to the people. His was one of the most engaging personalities it has ever been my good fortune to meet."[17]

Emmeline Blanch Wells also recorded her experience emigrating from England, coming up the Mississippi River and meeting Joseph Smith at the landing near his home in Nauvoo:

At last the boat reached the upper landing, and a crowd of people were coming toward the bank of the river. As we stepped ashore the crowd advanced, and I could see one person who towered away and above all the others around him; in fact I did not see distinctly any others. His majestic bearing, so entirely different from anyone I had ever seen (and I had seen many superior men) was more than a surprise. It was as if I beheld a vision; I seemed to be lifted off my feet, to be as it were walking in the air, and paying no heed whatever to those around me. I made my way through the crowd, then I saw this man whom I had noticed, because of his lofty appearance, shaking hands with all the people, men, women and children. Before I was aware of it he came to me, and when he took my hand, I was simply electrified,—thrilled through and through to the tips of my fingers, and every part of my body, as if some magic elixir had given me new life and vitality. I am sure that for a few minutes I was not conscious of motion. I think I stood still, I did not want to speak, or be spoken to. I was overwhelmed with indefinable emotion.[18]

The Prophet Joseph's countenance was a pleasing one to look upon. Bathsheba W. Smith gave us this description of him: "The Prophet was a handsome man,—splendid looking, a large man, tall and fair and his hair was light. He had a very nice complexion, his eyes were blue, and his hair a golden brown and very pretty. I have heard the Prophet Joseph preach many a time."[19]

Mary Alice Cannon Lambert described the affection the Saints felt for Joseph: "The love the Saints had for him was inexpressible. They would willingly have laid down their lives for him. If he was to talk, every task would be laid aside that they might listen to his words. He was not an ordinary man. Saints and sinners alike felt and recognized a power and influence which he carried with him. It was impossible to meet him and not be impressed by the strength of his personality and influence."[20]

One major reason why they loved him is because he loved them. His love for children is legendary. James W. Phippen recalled: "I have seen him on the playground with 'the boys,' as he called them, ball playing, wrestling, jumping, and helping to roll up logs on buildings for the widows. I have seen him in public and in private talking with the Saints on various occasions, so kind, so charitable, a Prophet in very deed, so noble in appearance. He loved the Saints. He was willing to suffer for them and die if necessary. Old members of the Church never tire of talking of Joseph, what he said and did. May his memory be fresh in their minds forever and with the children of the Saints."[21]

Joseph had implicit faith in the prayers of children for him. William Somerville, who served as a body guard to the Prophet, recalled a time when the prayers of children protected Joseph from harm. During a tense time in Nauvoo, William would lie on the floor with his feet placed up against the door of the bedroom of Joseph Smith's home where Joseph slept. Anyone attempting to enter the room would have to push the door against William and awaken him before they could get to the Prophet. "On one occasion, while on a guard duty assignment, the Prophet came to him and told him that on that particular night his guard service would not be needed, as it had been revealed to him that the little children had been praying for his welfare and the Lord had heard their prayers and would honor their faith by protecting him."[22]

Joseph was filled with kindness and generosity for others. In a letter to Edward Hunter, dated January 5, 1842, Joseph wrote about opening his red brick store in Nauvoo and how he could not help himself from serving the Saints: "The store has been filled to overflowing, and I have stood behind the counter all day, distributing goods, as steadily as any clerk you ever saw, to oblige those who were compelled to go without their Christmas and New Year's dinners, for the want of a little sugar, molasses, raisins, etc.; and to please myself also, for I love to wait upon the Saints, and to be a servant to all, hoping that I may be exalted in the due time of the Lord."[23]

A PERSON OF SIGNIFICANT ACCOMPLISHMENT

Besides his vibrant personality, Joseph was also a person of great accomplishment. With only a few years of elementary education, Joseph became a self-educated man and a great proponent of education. He formed adult education programs, missionary training schools, and established university level courses of study in Kirtland, Ohio, and procured a charter for a university at Nauvoo, Illinois.[24] He believed that "all the minds and spirits that God ever sent into the world are susceptible of enlargement."[25] He taught the Saints that "it is impossible for a man to be saved in ignorance" (D&C 131:6). He believed that education has an eternal impact and that "whatever principle of intelligence we attain unto in this life, it will rise with us in the resurrection. And if a person gains more knowledge and intelligence in this life through his diligence and obedience than another, he will have so much the advantage in the world to come" (D&C 130:18–19).

Thus, Joseph learned that "obedience" to God's commandments enables us to advance in spiritual understanding (intelligence), just as "diligent" effort enables us to grow intellectually (in knowledge).

Joseph was a translator of languages, including being among the first to translate a complete book from an ancient Egyptian text.[26] He also learned Hebrew, Greek, and German. He once remarked, "I am determined to pursue the study of language, until I shall become master of them, if I am permitted to live long enough."[27]

Joseph was a developer of a number of cities. He designed and planned the city of Zion at Independence, Missouri. He planned and organized the city of Nauvoo, which grew to be one of the largest cities in Illinois at the time.

Numerous other cities throughout the western United States (including Salt Lake City) are patterned after his design. In 1996, he was given an award posthumously by the 30,000-member American Planning Association for his vision in creating a city design plan that placed a high value on urban environment and development of a coherent community that provided social interaction, and that was proven to be agriculturally sustainable.[28]

The Prophet Joseph was the lieutenant general of the Nauvoo Legion—a militia of about 3,000 enlistees. To receive this honor, he was chosen by a vote of the people and commissioned by the governor of Illinois. He also led Zion's Camp, a military march from Ohio to Missouri. The organization he established in Zion's Camp was later replicated by President Brigham Young in the great exodus of the Saints to the Rocky Mountains.

At the time of his death, Joseph Smith was the mayor of Nauvoo, Illinois, and a candidate for the presidency of the United States. Several of his campaign proposals about how best to help his country are still issues today (such as prison reform and the number of elected representatives and the salary of those serving in Congress). If Joseph had been elected and his platform implemented, it could have dramatically altered American history. For example, one of his platforms called for the federal government to sell public lands to private citizens and use the money raised to purchase the freedom of all slaves. His plan was to abolish slavery by 1850.[29] The socio-economic impact of his visionary leadership would have been astounding.

Leo Tolstoy, a Russian historian, visited America in 1892 and was asked by a reporter, "In your study of great Americans this past year, who do you consider the greatest?" His answer, "You have only had one truly great American, one man gave to the world ideas that could change the whole destiny of the human race—Joseph Smith, the Mormon prophet."[30]

Joseph was an extraordinary man who possessed great strength of character, but that is not what qualified him to carry the appellation of "prophet." He was designated as such in a revelation from the Savior revealed the very day The Church of Jesus Christ of Latter-day Saints was organized: "Behold . . . thou shalt be called a seer, . . . a prophet, an apostle of Jesus Christ, . . . through the will of God the Father, and the grace of your Lord Jesus Christ" (D&C 21:1). Joseph Smith was a person of great strength, but the Church he founded was not built on him, nor did its success rest on his personality. Some thought that the Church would come to an end with the death of Joseph Smith, but Joseph testified: "I obtained power on the principles of truth and virtue, which would last when I was dead and gone."[31] The work Joseph Smith established is greater than the Prophet Joseph himself because it is God's work.

Notes

1. "Joseph Smith, the Prophet," *Historical Record* (January 1888): 576.

2. Lucy Mack Smith, *History of Joseph Smith by His Mother Lucy Mack Smith* (Salt Lake City: Bookcraft, 1958), 254–56.

3. In Neal A. Maxwell, *We Talk of Christ, We Rejoice in Christ* (Salt Lake City: Deseret Book, 1984), 86.

4. In Conference Reports of The Church of Jesus Christ of Latter-day Saints (Salt Lake City: The Church of Jesus Christ of Latter-day Saints, 1898 to present), October 1897, 64; *Elders' Journal* 1, no. 4 (August 1838), 51, as cited in Matthew B. Brown, *Joseph Smith: The Man, The Mission, The Message* (American Fork, Utah: Covenant Communications, 2004), 26.

5. As cited in Brown, *Joseph Smith: The Man, the Mission, the Message*, 26.

6. Benjamin F. Johnson, *My Life's Review* (Mesa, Arizona: 21st

Century Printing, 1992), 92–93.

7. As cited in Joseph Quinney, in Conference Reports, April 1924, 127.

8. As cited in John Henry Evans, *Joseph Smith, An American Prophet* (Salt Lake City: Deseret Book, 1966), 4.

9. *The Religious, Social, and Political History of the Mormons or Latter-day Saints from Their Origins to the Present Time*, ed. Samuel M. Smucker (New York: Miller, Orton and Company, 1857), 183.

10. *New York Sun*, 4 September 1843.

11. Joseph Smith, *History of The Church of Jesus Christ of Latter-day Saints*, ed. B. H. Roberts, 2d ed. rev., 7 vols. (Salt Lake City: The Church of Jesus Christ of Latter-day Saints, 1980), 5:498.

12. Ibid., 5:498.

13. Ibid., 2:229.

14. Joseph Smith, *Teachings of the Prophet Joseph Smith*, comp. Joseph Fielding Smith (Salt Lake City: Deseret Book, 1976), 361–62.

15. Thomas S. Monson, "How Do We Show Our Love?" *Ensign*, January 1998, 2.

16. Jane Manning James, "Joseph Smith, the Prophet," *Young Woman's Journal* (1905): 551–52.

17. Jane Snyder Richards, "Joseph Smith, the Prophet," *Young Woman's Journal* (1905): 550.

18. Emmeline Blanch Wells, "Joseph Smith, the Prophet," *Young Woman's Journal* (1905): 555.

19. Bathsheba W. Smith, "Joseph Smith, the Prophet," *Young Woman's Journal* (1905): 549.

20. Mary Alice Cannon Lambert, "Joseph Smith, the Prophet," *Young Woman's Journal* (1905): 554.

21. James W. Phippen, "Joseph Smith, the Prophet," *Young Woman's Journal* (1906): 540.

22. As cited in Mark L. McConkie, *Remembering Joseph* (Salt Lake City: Deseret Book, 2003), 116–17.

23. George Q. Cannon, *The Life of Joseph Smith, the Prophet* (Salt Lake City: Deseret Book, 1986), 386.

24. Of this university, Joseph declared, it "will enable us to teach our children wisdom, to instruct them in all the knowledge and learning, in the arts, sciences, and learned professions. We hope to make this institution one of the great lights of the world, and by and through it to diffuse that kind of knowledge which will be of

practicable utility, and for the public good, and also for private and individual happiness" (*History of the Church*, 4:269).

25. Smith, *History of the Church*, 6:311.

26. The Book of Mormon was written in "reformed Egyptian" (Mormon 9:32).

27. Smith, *History of the Church*, 2:396.

28. An 1833 "'Plat of Zion,' Wins National Honor," *Church News*, 25 May 1996, 11.

29. *Church History in the Fulness of Times*, Institute Student Manual, prepared by the Church Educational System (Salt Lake City: The Church of Jesus Christ of Latter-day Saints, 1989), 269–70.

30. As reported by William E. Berrett, "The Life and Character of the Prophet Joseph Smith," *BYU Speeches of the Year* (Provo: Brigham Young University Press), 21 April 1964, 2.

31. *Presidents of the Church*, Institute Student Manual, prepared by the Church Educational System (Salt Lake City: The Church of Jesus Christ of Latter-day Saints, 1979), 25.

CHAPTER FOUR

THE RESTORATION CAME THROUGH, NOT FROM, THE PROPHET JOSEPH SMITH

As early as March 1829, the Lord declared to the Prophet Joseph Smith: "This generation shall have my word *through* you" (D&C 5:10; emphasis added). At the time Joseph Smith was twenty-three years of age. He would only live fifteen more years. But in those fifteen very compressed years, Joseph Smith became the instrument through whom the Lord ushered in the final "dispensation of the fulness of times" in which all things "from the days of Adam even to the present time . . . shall be revealed" (D&C 128:18, 20–21).

Note that the Lord said the Restoration would come *through*—not *from* or *by*—the Prophet Joseph Smith (D&C 5:10). The Restoration was so grand in vision, so all-encompassing in thought and doctrine, so beyond mortal power and authority that it could not possibly have come *from* the Prophet Joseph or *from* any other individual. Since the death of the original apostles, no person, no committee, no council, and no creed had been able to bring back the original Church with all its doctrines, priesthoods, and principles. Many have recognized that things have been missing. But no individual, nor any group of individuals, were ever able to recover what was lost. The work of the Restoration was simply beyond human ability. It required direct revelation from God.

Even if Joseph Smith had been the most gifted linguist,

the most learned biblical scholar, the most studied anthro-
pologist, the most spiritual intellect on the face of the earth
(which I believe he was), he still would not have been able
to restore the priesthood keys and authority that had been
taken from the earth with the death of the early apostles.
Priesthood authority can only be given by the laying on of
hands by someone holding the proper authority. That is why
Daniel, Peter, John the Beloved, and other prophets foretold
of the need for a latter-day restoration from heaven.[1]

What do we have today that we would not have without
the Prophet Joseph Smith? In a word—everything—including a correct understanding of God the Father, His Son,
Jesus Christ; the doctrines, principles and ordinances of
the gospel; the authority of the holy priesthood; and the
hundreds of pages of scripture and modern revelation he
revealed and restored.

We honor him, we value his teachings, we revere him
as a prophet called of God, and we therefore afford him the
greatest respect, but we do not worship Joseph Smith, as
some may naively assume. In fact, a great many members of
the Church that Joseph Smith founded do not even know
where he is buried. (His final resting place is located in
Nauvoo, Illinois.) President Gordon B. Hinckley observed:
"We do not worship the prophet. We worship God, our
Eternal Father, and the risen Lord Jesus Christ. But we
acknowledge him. . . . We reverence him as an instrument
in the hands of the Almighty in restoring to the earth the
ancient truths of the divine gospel, together with the priesthood through which the authority of God is exercised in the
affairs of his church and for the blessing of his people."[2]

As mentioned earlier, all of the presidents of The Church
of Jesus Christ of Latter-day Saints have been and are
prophets, seers, and revelators, but the title "The Prophet"
uniquely refers to the Prophet Joseph Smith. "Latter-day

Saints call him 'the Prophet' because, in the tradition of Old and New Testament prophets, he depended on revelation from God for his teachings, not on his own learning."[3] We believe that he received revelations from God to perform a work for the salvation of souls that is greater than any other individual's except that of our Lord and Savior Jesus Christ (D&C 135:3). The Church that Joseph Smith was inspired to restore was revealed from heaven. It was not something Joseph conceived in counsel with others. It has been built up by the power of God to be a light, standard, and messenger to prepare the world for the second coming of Jesus Christ (D&C 45:9). It did not originate with Joseph Smith, nor did it end when he was martyred.

THE MANTLE OF HIS CALLING

Understanding Joseph Smith's brilliance is an enigma to people who refuse to accept him as a prophet called of God. His religious training came not from books, nor from great halls of learning in Ivy-covered universities, nor from studying the tomes of the learned, but at the feet of angelic beings.[4] He had only a rudimentary education by the world's standards, but he had a mind and a spirit that comprehended all eternity. His limited opportunities for secular education did not hinder him because he was heaven-taught and angel-tutored. Though he never earned a degree from a worldly university, he earned a PhD from the University of Kolob! He knew more about divine truths and revealed religion than anyone else on earth. He observed that "reading the experience of others . . . can never give us a comprehensive view of our condition and true relation to God. Knowledge of these things can only be obtained by experience through the ordinances of God set forth for that purpose. *Could you gaze into heaven five minutes, you would know more than you would by reading all that ever was written on the subject.*"[5] And Joseph was blessed, many times, to have that opportunity. His knowledge of spiritual things was unbounded. In his great King Follett Discourse, given to the Saints in Nauvoo just shortly before his martyrdom, Joseph declared, "I am learned, and know more than all the world put together. The Holy Ghost does, anyhow, and he is within me, and comprehends more than all the world; and I will associate myself with him."[6]

Joseph Smith's eternal education began in his home, with a family who taught him to read and believe in the scriptures and to trust God and pray to Him in faith. The prophesied restitution "of all things, which God hath spoken by the mouth of all his holy prophets since the world began" was launched with the prayer of this young boy living in upstate New York in 1820 (Acts 3:19-21). Joseph went into the woods near his home to ask a simple question, "Which of all the churches was true, which should I join?" As he prayed in faith, a light appeared above him and gradually descended until it filled the area around him with great light. He said, "When the light rested upon me I saw two Personages, whose brightness and glory defy all description, standing above me in the air. One of them spake unto me, calling me by name and said, pointing to the other—This is My Beloved Son. Hear Him!" (Joseph Smith–History 1:17). Imagine how much one could learn from such personal moments with the Father and the Son. Truly, Joseph knew more about God than any other person on earth. He was told to join none of the existing churches in his day, but that the fullness of the Gospel of Jesus Christ would be restored through him.

Reflecting on his experiences, Joseph later observed: "Knowledge through our Lord and Savior Jesus Christ is the grand key that unlocks the glories and mysteries of the kingdom of heaven."[7] Joseph could say that because he knew the Lord personally. Imagine being tutored by the very God who created the known universe. The prophet Moses had the same experience and afterward exclaimed, "Now . . . I know that man is nothing, which thing I never had supposed" (Moses 1:10). All the accumulated knowledge of humankind pales in comparison to God's understanding.

Elder Daniel H. Wells, who joined the Church after living among the Saints in Nauvoo for some time, testified of what a privilege it was to know Joseph and how impressive his understanding of heavenly things was. He said he "frequently heard him speak; and, though I did not at first believe that he was inspired or that he was more than a man of great natural ability, I soon learned that he knew more about religion and the things of God and eternity than any man I had ever heard talk . . . and it seemed to me that he advanced principles that neither he nor any other man could have obtained except from the Source of all wisdom—the Lord himself. I soon discovered that he was not what the world termed a well-read or an educated man; then where could he have got this knowledge and understanding, that so far surpassed all I had ever witnessed, unless it had come from Heaven?"[8]

Three years following his First Vision, the Lord sent the angel Moroni to Joseph Smith to further prepare his heart and mind for the restoration of the gospel of Jesus Christ to the earth. Within a twenty-four-hour period on September 21–22, 1823, Moroni appeared five times to Joseph (Joseph Smith–History 1:29–53). It was the fall equinox; a new season was about to begin on the earth and in Joseph's life. One of Moroni's instructions on the Hill Cumorah to Joseph was for him to return the following year to receive "intelligence . . . respecting what the Lord was going to do, and how and in what manner his kingdom was to be conducted in the last days" (Joseph Smith–History 1:54). Their meetings continued for the next four years. During these four years, it was as though Moroni (a soldier and leader of Nephite armies during his lifetime; Mormon 6:2) had put Joseph through a spiritual boot camp. Moroni's guidance and teachings during Joseph's teenage years were spiritually strengthening. As a result, Joseph never doubted his experiences or flinched in his resolve to follow the Lord the rest of his life despite the obstacles and intense opposition that hounded him.

Later, as Joseph read and translated the Bible, other angelic beings were sent to minister to him. Thus, Joseph Smith not only read and studied the Bible, he also knew its authors! He was personally tutored by many of them on numerous occasions.[9] President George Q. Cannon testified: "He . . . received the ministration of divers angels—heads of dispensations—from Michael or Adam down to the present time; every man in his time and season coming to him, and all declaring their dispensation, their rights, their keys, their honors . . . [H]e received from all these different sources all the power and all the authority and all keys that were necessary for the building up of the work of God in the last days."[10] John Taylor once commented, "If you were to ask Joseph what sort of a looking man Adam was, he would tell you at once; he would tell you his size and appearance and all about him. You might have asked him what sort of men Peter, James, and John were, and he could have told you. Why? Because he had seen them."[11] Joseph Bates Noble said, "In 1833 I went to Kirtland where I saw for the first time Joseph Smith. I went with him to a field and helped him mow some hay. While there he gave me much information in relation to the Book of Mormon, etc. etc. He told me that the voices of the angels became so familiar that he knew their names before he saw them."[12] John Taylor furthered testified, "The principles which he had placed him in communication with the Lord, and not only with the Lord, but with the ancient apostles and prophets: such men, for instance, as Abraham, Isaac, Jacob, Noah, Adam, Seth, Enoch, and Jesus, and the Father, and the apostles that lived on this continent, as well as those who lived on the Asiatic continent. He seemed to be as familiar with these people as we are with one another. Why? Because he had to introduce a dispensation which was called the dispensation of the fullness of times, and it was known as such by the ancient servants of God."[13]

Additionally, as prophet, seer, and revelator, Joseph Smith made hundreds of prophesies, many of which have come to pass while many others have yet to be fulfilled. When Moroni appeared to him, Joseph was a seventeen-year-old boy in an obscure village. Moroni announced that "God had a work for me to do; . . . that my name should be had for good and evil among all nations, kindreds, and tongues, or that it should be both good and evil spoken of among all people" (Joseph Smith–History 1:33). As reported by Oliver Cowdery, the angel Moroni said, "Your name shall be known among the nations, for the work which the Lord will perform by your hands shall cause the righteous to rejoice and the wicked to rage; with the one it shall be had in honor, and with the other in reproach; yet, with these it shall be a terror because of the great and marvelous work which shall follow the coming forth of this fulness of the gospel."[14]

Consider the implications of such prophetic statements coming from a seventeen-year-old, inconspicuous farm boy living in the nineteenth century. What are the chances that such a prophecy could possibly come to pass given the time and place he lived? Even with our modern technological abilities and advanced communications, how would it be possible for that prophesy to be fulfilled in "all nations" without divine help? Yet, just as Moroni foresaw, there are thousands of books, pamphlets, and articles about Joseph Smith in many languages over most of the earth. Moroni's prophecy has been and will continue to be fulfilled.

The Restoration was not a product of Joseph Smith's imagination. It is the work of the Lord, and it has been established in these latter days to bless the entire human family (1 Nephi 15:18; 45:9–10).

President Wilford Woodruff was present at the last speech Joseph ever gave the Twelve Apostles before the Martyrdom, when Joseph told them that he had received and passed to them all the authority he had been given so that the Church could continue to grow and thrive. He said,

> I have had sealed upon my head every key, every power, every principle of life and salvation that God has ever given to any man who ever lived upon the face of the earth. And these principles and this Priesthood and power belong to this great and last dispensation which the God of Heaven has set His hand to establish in the earth. Now, . . . I have sealed upon your heads every key, every power, and every principle which the Lord has sealed upon my head. . . . I tell you, the burden of this kingdom now rests upon your shoulders; you have got to bear it off [build it up] in all the world."[15]

Under the direction of the First Presidency the and Twelve Apostles, the foundation Joseph laid continues to be built up at an accelerated pace. Who but inspired prophets could have envisioned such a global organization so many years ago? Even those who helped found the Church were not, at first, fully aware of what would result. After listening to the testimonies of several leading brethren assembled in a small room in Kirtland, Ohio, the Prophet Joseph declared, "I have been very much edified and instructed in your testimonies here tonight, but I want to say to you before the Lord, that you know no more concerning the destinies of this Church and kingdom than a babe upon its mother's lap. You don't comprehend it. It is only a little handful of Priesthood you see here tonight, but this Church will fill North and South America. It will fill the world."[16] It is coming to pass as he and other prophets have foreseen (1 Nephi 14:12).

GREATNESS OF JOSEPH SMITH'S MISSION AND MESSAGE

When the angel Moroni visited Joseph, he told him "that God had a work for [him] to do" (Joseph Smith–History 1:33). He also quoted numerous scriptures about the last days which he declared "were about to be fulfilled"[17] and then added a warning: "The workers of iniquity will seek your overthrow: they will circulate falsehoods to destroy your reputation, and also will seek to take your life." Even so, Moroni reassured Joseph that the great work restored through him would "increase the more [it was] opposed."[18]

The work was opposed, and Joseph and his family were often persecuted. President Brigham Young later commented, "If a thousand hounds were on this Temple Block [Temple Square in Salt Lake City], let loose on one rabbit, it would not be a bad illustration of the situation at times of the Prophet Joseph. He was hunted unremittingly."[19]

At one point, Joseph wondered if he would ever live to complete the work God had called him to do. It must have seemed so overwhelming to him. On his father's deathbed, Joseph Smith Sr. promised his son Joseph, "You shall live even to finish your work." According to Lucy Mack Smith, her son "cried out, weeping, 'Oh! my Father, shall I?' 'Yes,' said his father, 'you shall live to lay out the plan of all the work which God has given you to do. This is my dying blessing upon your head in the name of Jesus . . . for it shall be fulfilled.'"[20]

He learned by revelation that he would not be sacrificed until his mission was completed:

> God Almighty is my shield; and what can man do if God is my friend? I shall not be sacrificed until my time comes; then I shall be offered freely.[21]

> God will always protect me until my mission is fulfilled.[22]

> I prophesy they never will have power to kill me till my work is accomplished, and I am ready to die.[23]

Joseph had faith that God would bless him, but it did not make his life any less stressful. Joseph commented on the primary reason for the severe persecution against him: "When I went home and told the people that I had a revelation, and that all the churches were corrupt, they persecuted me, and they have persecuted me ever since."[24] His brother William commented that their family was well respected in the community until Joseph announced he had seen God. After that, William reports, their family's reputation was of the worst kind.[25] Brigham Young observed, "Why was he hunted from neighborhood to neighborhood, from city to city, and from State to State, and at last suffered death? Because he received revelations from the Father, from the Son, and was ministered to by holy angels, and published to the world the direct will of the Lord concerning his children on the earth."[26]

Joseph Smith declared to the world that he had seen God, that God is an exalted man, that we are created in God's very image, and that as His eternal offspring, we can eventually become like Him. This testimony, born by all true prophets in ages past, has cost the best blood of the earth (Mosiah 7:27–28; Helaman 13:26–29), and it likewise cost Joseph Smith his life.

BLESSINGS FROM UNDER HIS HAND

Significantly, however, the angel Moroni had also declared to Joseph Smith that despite the opposition he would encounter, not all would be lost—that there would be individuals among "all nations, kindreds, and tongues" who would speak well of him (Joseph Smith–History 1:33). Fourteen years later, when Joseph was unjustly incarcerated in a filthy dungeon in Liberty, Missouri, the Savior reiterated Moroni's promise: "The ends of the earth shall inquire after thy name, and fools shall have thee in derision, and hell shall rage against thee; *While the pure in heart, and the wise, and the noble, and the virtuous, shall seek counsel, and authority, and blessings constantly from under thy hand. And thy people shall never be turned against thee by the testimony of traitors.* And although their influence shall cast thee into trouble, and into bars and walls, thou shalt be had in honor . . . and thy God shall stand by thee forever and ever" (D&C 122:1–3; emphasis added). Joseph was further promised, "The Holy Ghost shall be thy constant companion, and thy scepter an unchanging scepter of righteousness and truth; and thy dominion shall be an everlasting dominion . . . [which shall] flow unto thee forever and ever" (D&C 121:46). Today, millions across the earth bear witness of the Prophet Joseph

Smith and testify that they have received counsel, authority, and have obtained eternal blessings because of Joseph Smith's life and teachings.

JOSEPH HOLDS THE KEYS OF THIS FINAL DISPENSATION

Throughout human history there are only a handful of individuals who have had as much written about them, both pro and con, as the Prophet Joseph Smith. I believe that every individual who writes about him will one day have to account to him for their writings. There are reasons for this. Joseph Smith, although slain as a martyr, still lives beyond the veil and continues to stand at the head of the final dispensation of the gospel on the earth. President Ezra Taft Benson said the Prophet Joseph "will continue so to stand [in that position of authority] throughout the eternities to come."[27] The hymn "Praise to the Man" echoes this same sentiment with these words:

> Great is his glory and endless his priesthood.
> Ever and ever the keys he will hold.
> Faithful and true, he will enter his kingdom,
> Crowned in the midst of the prophets of
> old.[28]

Joseph Smith received all the keys to the "dispensation of the fullness of times" (D&C 112:30) and was chosen to preside over the "times of restitution of all things, which God hath spoken by the mouth of all his holy prophets since the world began" (Acts 3:21), when all things will be gathered together "in Christ, both which are in heaven, and which are on earth" (Ephesians 1:10). The Prophet Joseph was the individual called to oversee the final winding up scene "for the last days and for the last time" (D&C 112:30)—the time when nothing would be withheld, when God would reveal knowledge through living prophets by the "unspeakable gift of the Holy Ghost, that has not been revealed since the world was until now; which our forefathers [the ancient prophets] have awaited with anxious expectation to be revealed in the last times . . . according to that which was ordained in the midst of the Council of the Eternal God" in order that every person could enter into God's "eternal presence and into his immortal rest" (D&C 121:26-27, 32).

This places Joseph Smith in a unique place among all the prophets of the earth. President George Q. Cannon said:

> He [Joseph Smith], therefore, received the ministration of divers angels—heads of dispensations—from Michael or Adam down to the present time; every man in his time and season coming to him, and all declaring their dispensation, their rights, their keys, their honors, their majesty and glory, and the power of their Priesthood. So that Joseph, the head of this dispensation, Prophet, Seer and Revelator, whom God raised up, received from all these different sources, according to the mind and will of God, and according to the design of God concerning him; he received from all these different sources all the power and all the authority and all keys that were necessary for the building up of the work of God in the last days, and for the accomplishment of His purposes connected with this dispensation. He stands at the head. He is a unique character, differing from every other man in this respect, and excelling every other man.[29]

Joseph Smith was chosen—foreknown, forecalled, and foreordained—of God, to speak to the world this final time. What is it that makes our dispensation different from all others? Ours is the *last* dispensation before the Second Coming. Ours is the dispensation of gathering, linking, and uniting all that has preceded us. Our message is critical for all to hear because the eternal salvation of every soul rests upon the shoulders of the Church of Jesus Christ restored through Joseph Smith. If the world is going to be saved, we have to do it. The mandate given to the Latter-day Saints is to see that all who are now living (or who will yet be born) hear the message of the Restoration and that all who have ever lived have temple ordinances performed in their behalf.

In fact, the Lord declared that if the message of the restored gospel, the testimony of Christ's atoning sacrifice and resurrection, and the sacred ordinances of the temple are not taken to every nation, kindred, tongue, and people, "the whole earth [would] be smitten with a curse and utterly wasted at his coming [the Savior's second coming]" (D&C 138:48; 2:1–3). Simply put, the gospel of Jesus Christ, as revealed to Joseph Smith, will save the world. This everlasting covenant, restored in our day, is the "power to obtain eternal life" and is the light, the standard, and the messenger sent "to prepare the way before me," the Savior said, and then invitingly declared, "Wherefore, come ye unto it" (D&C 45:8–10).

Thus, Joseph Smith's testimony and his prophetic utterances comprise the greatest message to all mankind in these latter days. With such an important message, little wonder the adversary battled so incessantly against the Prophet Joseph throughout his entire life. From the time of his First Vision to his martyrdom twenty-four years later, the Prophet Joseph worked tirelessly to bring the world God's truth. Even those who fail to revere Joseph Smith as the Lord's mouth-piece will one day realize the greatness of his call from God: "You call us fools," President Heber C. Kimball said, "but the day will be, gentlemen and ladies, whether you belong to this Church or not, when you will prize brother Joseph Smith as the Prophet of the Living God."[30]

Shortly after the Prophet Joseph Smith's death at Carthage, the Quorum of the Twelve issued a proclamation to the world from Nauvoo about the restoration of the gospel, thus fulfilling an assignment given by revelation five years earlier to "make a solemn proclamation of my gospel . . . to all the kings of the world, to the four corners thereof, and to all the nations of the earth" (D&C 124:2-3). In this proclamation they said:

> Know ye:
> That the kingdom of God has come: as has been predicted by ancient prophets, and prayed for in all ages; even that kingdom which shall fill the whole earth, and shall stand for ever.
>
> The great Eloheem . . . has been pleased once more to speak from the heavens: and also to commune with man upon the earth, by means of open visions, and by the ministration of Holy Messengers.
>
> By this means the great and eternal High Priesthood, after the Order of His Son, even the Apostleship, has been restored; or, returned to the earth.
>
> This High Priesthood, or Apostleship, holds the keys of the kingdom of God, and power to bind on earth that which shall be bound in heaven; and to loose on earth that which shall be loosed in heaven. And, in fine, to do, and to administer in all things pertaining

to the ordinances, organization, government and direction of the kingdom of God.

Being established in these last days for the restoration of all things spoken by the prophets since the world began; and in order to prepare the way for the coming of the Son of Man.

And we now bear witness that his coming is near at hand; and not many years hence, the nations and their kings shall see him coming in the clouds of heaven with power and great glory.[31]

This proclamation continues by declaring, "As this work progresses in its onward course, and becomes more and more an object of political and religious interest . . . no king, ruler, or subject, no community or individual, will stand neutral. All will . . . be influenced by one spirit or the other; and will take sides either for or against the kingdom of God."[32]

Thus, Moroni's prophecy to Joseph Smith that his name would be had for good or evil among all nations will continue to find fulfillment.

Notes

1. Daniel 2:34; Acts 3:19–21; Revelation 14:6–7; cf. D&C 27:6, 13–14 and 128:19–21.

2. Gordon B. Hinckley, "Joseph the Seer," *Ensign*, May 1977, 65.

3. *Encyclopedia of Mormonism*, 4 vols., ed. Daniel H. Ludlow (New York: Macmillan, 1992), 3:1331.

4. H. Donl Peterson, *Moroni, Ancient Prophet, Modern Messenger* (Salt Lake City: Deseret Book, 2000), 132–34, 148–50.

5. Joseph Smith, *Teachings of the Prophet Joseph Smith*, comp. Joseph Fielding Smith (Salt Lake City: Deseret Book, 1976), 324.

6. Ibid., 350.

7. Ibid., 298.

8. Daniel H. Wells, in *Journal of Discourses*, 26 vols. (London: Latter-day Saints' Book Depot, 1854–86), 12:72–73.

9. W. Jeffrey Marsh, "A Mission Long Foreknown," *Ensign*, January 2001, 30. To see a list of the ancient apostles and prophets who visited and ministered to Joseph Smith, see H. Donl Peterson, *Moroni, Ancient Prophet, Modern Messenger* (Salt Lake City: Deseret Book, 2000), 132–34, 148–50.

10. George Q. Cannon, in *Journal of Discourses*, 23:361.

11. John Taylor, in *Journal of Discourses*, 18:326.

12. Joseph Bates Noble, *A Journal or Diary of Joseph Bates Noble 1810–1834* (L. Tom Perry Special Collections, Harold B. Lee Library, Brigham Young University, Provo, Utah), 3.

13. John Taylor, in *Journal of Discourses*, 17:374–75.

14. B. H. Roberts, *Comprehensive History of The Church of Jesus Christ of Latter-day Saints*, 6 vols. (Salt Lake City: Deseret News Press, 1930), 1:80.

15. J. M. Whitacker, "Priesthood and the Rights of Succession," *Deseret News Weekly* (19 March 1892): 406.

16. Wilford Woodruff, in Conference Reports of The Church of Jesus Christ of Latter-day Saints (Salt Lake City: The Church of Jesus Christ of Latter-day Saints, 1898 to present), April 1898, 57.

17. To read more about the verses quoted by Moroni to Joseph Smith, see Kent P. Jackson, "Moroni's Message to Joseph Smith," *Ensign*, August 1990, 13; and W. Jeffrey Marsh, "Training from the Old Testament: Moroni's Lessons for a Prophet," *Ensign*, August 1998, 10.

18. Oliver Cowdery, "Letter VIII," *Messenger and Advocate* (October 1835): 199; as cited in Joseph Fielding McConkie, *Answers: Straightforward Answers to Tough Gospel Questions* (Salt Lake City: Deseret Book, 1998), 53–54.

19. *Discourses of Brigham Young*, ed. John A. Widtsoe (Salt Lake City: Deseret Book, 1954), 464.

20. Lucy Mack Smith, *History of Joseph Smith by His Mother Lucy Mack Smith* (Salt Lake City: Bookcraft, 1958), 309–10.

21. Joseph Smith, *History of The Church of Jesus Christ of Latter-day Saints*, ed. B. H. Roberts, 2d ed. rev., 7 vols. (Salt Lake City: The Church of Jesus Christ of Latter-day Saints, 1980), 5:259.

22. Smith, *Teachings*, 366.

23. Smith, *History of the Church*, 6:58.

24. As cited in Milton V. Backman Jr., *Joseph Smith's First Vision: Confirming Evidences and Contemporary Accounts*, 2d ed. (Salt Lake

City: Bookcraft, 1980), 176.

25. As cited in "Joseph Smith's New York Reputation Reappraised," by Richard Lloyd Anderson, *BYU Studies* (Spring 1970): 313.

26. As cited in "A Mission Long Foreknown," *Ensign*, January 2001, 33.

27. Ezra Taft Benson, "A Message to the World," *Ensign*, May 1975, 34.

28. *Hymns of The Church of Jesus Christ of Latter-day Saints* (Salt Lake City: The Church of Jesus Christ of Latter-day Saints, 1985), no. 27.

29. George Q. Cannon, in *Journal of Discourses*, 23:361–62

30. Heber C. Kimball, in *Journal of Discourses*, 5:88.

31. "1845 Proclamation of the Twelve," as cited in *Messages of the First Presidency of The Church of Jesus Christ of Latter-day Saints*, 6 vols., ed. James R. Clark (Salt Lake City: Bookcraft, 1965–75), 1:253.

32. As cited by Ezra Taft Benson, "May the Kingdom of God Go Forth," *Ensign*, May 1978, 32.

CHAPTER FIVE

THE EDUCATION OF THE PROPHET

Howard Coray, a clerk to the Prophet, noted how brilliant Joseph's ideas were while he conversed with others:

> While I was employed in this manner, I had many valuable opportunities. The Prophet had a great many callers and visitors, and he received them in his office where I was clerking, persons of almost all professions— doctors, lawyers, priests, and people anxious to get a good look at what was then considered to be something very wonderful—a man who should dare to call himself a prophet, announce himself as a seer and ambassador of the Lord. Not only were they anxious to see, but also to ask hard questions in order to ascertain his depth. Well, what did I discover? This, verily, that he was always equal to the occasion and perfectly master of the situation and possessed the power to make everybody realize his superiority, which they evidenced in an unmistakable manner. I could clearly see that Joseph was the captain, no matter whose company he was in. Knowing the meagerness of his education, I was truly gratified at seeing how much at ease he always was, even in the company of the most scientific, and the ready, off-hand manner in which he would answer their questions.

Peter H. Burnett, an attorney who helped defend the Mormons during times of persecution and who later became the first governor of California, wrote this description of Joseph's native intelligence:

> He was much more than an ordinary man. He possessed the most indomitable perseverance, was a good judge of men, and deemed himself born to command, and he did command. His views were so strange and striking, and his manner was so earnest, and apparently so candid, that you could not but be interested. There was a kind, familiar look about him, that pleased you. He was very courteous in discussion, readily admitting what he did not intend to controvert, and would not oppose you abruptly, but had due deference to your feelings. He had the capacity for discussing a subject in different aspects, and for proposing many original views, even of ordinary matters. His illustrations were his own. He had great influence over others.[2]

Many loved to hear him preach. Reflecting on the experience of listening to Joseph teach, Brigham Young once said, "Such moments were more precious to me than all the wealth of the world. No matter how great my poverty—If I had to borrow meal to feed my wife and children, I never let an opportunity pass of learning what the prophet had to impart."[3] Brigham Young also commented: "What a delight it was to hear brother Joseph talk upon the great principles of eternity; he would bring them down to the capacity of a child, and he would unite heaven with earth, this is the beauty of our religion."[4]

Wandle Mace, an acquaintance and friend of the Prophet

Joseph Smith, said, "We were sure of a rare treat if we could get him to talk to us. Someone present being in a hurry to hear him would say, 'Brother Joseph talk to us.' He would say, 'What do you want me to talk about, start something.' Soon a conversation would bring out som[e] question for Joseph to answer, and then I could lean back and listen. Ah what pleasure this gave me; he would unravel the scriptures and explain doctrine as no other man could. What had been mystery he made so plain it was no longer mystery."[5]

A LIFELONG LEARNER

Joseph testified that spiritual growth, like intellectual attainment, is a line-upon-line experience based upon obedience to eternal principles: "We cannot expect to know all, or more than we now know unless we comply with or keep those we have already received."[6]

Joseph also understood that the process of coming to know what God knows, of becoming like Him, is not something that occurs overnight: "When you climb a ladder, you must begin at the bottom, and ascend step by step until you arrive at the top; and so it is with the principles of the Gospel: you must begin with the first, and go on until you learn all the principles of exaltation. But it will be a great while after you have passed through the vail [veil] before you will have learned them. It is not all to be comprehended in this world: it will be a great work to learn our salvation and exaltation even beyond the grave."[7] Indeed, it "will be a great while before you learn the last. It is not all to be comprehended in this world."[8]

Echoing the admonitions of Paul (Philippians 4:8), Joseph declared that one of the fundamental articles of our faith is to follow the injunction that "if there is anything virtuous, lovely, or of good report or praiseworthy, we seek after these things" (Article of Faith 13). Joseph was inspired to counsel the Saints to get all the learning and education possible: "And as all have not faith, seek ye diligently and teach one another words of wisdom; yea, seek ye out of the best books words of wisdom; seek learning, even by study and also by faith" (D&C 88:118).

Joseph saw an inseparable link between secular and spiritual education. He organized schools in every city he helped settle. "The disciples should lose no time in preparing schools for their children, that they may be taught as is pleasing unto the Lord, and brought up in the way of holiness. . . . It is all-important that children to become good should be taught [good]."[9] Joseph was quick to act on this counsel because the Lord had revealed that when we are striving to gain an education, we are about our Father's business. Pursuing an education is an endeavor worthy of our time and energy: "Verily I say unto you my friends, I speak unto you with my voice, even the voice of my Spirit, that I may show unto you my will concerning . . . [those who] are truly humble and are seeking diligently to learn wisdom and to find truth. Verily, verily I say unto you, blessed are such, for they shall obtain. . . . Behold, I say unto you, concerning the school in Zion, I, the Lord, am well pleased that there should be a school in Zion" (D&C 97:1–3).

The Saints were commanded to teach one another true doctrine and to do so diligently. They were promised that Christ's grace would attend their efforts (D&C 88:77–78). They were commanded to instruct one another "more perfectly in theory, in principle, in doctrine, in the law of the gospel, in all things that pertain unto the kingdom of God" (D&C 88:78). But they were not to limit their learning to spiritual things: "Teach ye diligently . . . of things both in heaven [astronomy] and in the earth [cultivation and proper use of soil], and under the earth [geology, mineralogy];

things which have been [history], things which are [current events], things which must shortly come to pass [prophecy and revelation]; things which are at home [domestic policy], things which are abroad [foreign policy]; the wars and perplexities of the nations, and the judgments which are on the land [signs of the times]; and a knowledge also of countries and of kingdoms [geography, languages, and so forth] (D&C 88:78–79).

Joseph noted that our educational endeavors will not end with this life. Our efforts to learn new things about our world will continue at an accelerated pace when the Savior returns at the time of His second coming: "Yea, verily I say unto you, in that day when the Lord shall come, he shall reveal all things—things which have passed, and hidden things which no man knew, things of the earth, by which it was made, and the purpose and the end thereof—Things most precious, things that are above, and things that are beneath, things that are in the earth, and upon the earth, and in heaven" (D&C 101:32–34).

What is the purpose of all this learning? Joseph Smith responded, to help us become like our Heavenly Father:

> We consider that God has created man with a mind capable of instruction, and a faculty which may be enlarged in proportion to the heed and diligence given to the light communicated from heaven to the intellect; and that the nearer man approaches perfection, the clearer are his views, and the greater his enjoyments, till he has overcome the evils of his life and lost every desire for sin; and like the ancients, arrives at that point of faith where he is wrapped in the power and glory of his Maker and is caught up to dwell with Him. But we consider that this is a station to

which no man ever arrived in a moment: he must have been instructed in the government and laws of that kingdom by proper degrees, until his mind is capable in some measure of comprehending the propriety, justice, equality, and consistency of the same.[10]

LIMITING OURSELVES

One of the challenges Joseph faced in trying to educate the Saints in the things of eternity was their unwillingness to receive light and truth. Ancient prophets faced the same dilemma, as Alma explained, they were "laid under a strict command that they shall not impart only according to the portion of his word which he doth grant unto the children of men, according to the heed and diligence which they give unto him" (Alma 12:9). Thus, we limit ourselves only by unworthiness or unpreparedness.

The Prophet Joseph observed that traditions and customs often held the Saints back from receiving what the Lord had to impart. He warned, "I say to all those who are disposed to set up stakes for the Almighty, You will come short of the glory of God. To become a joint heir of the heirship of the Son, one must put away all his false traditions."[11] He said it was almost like an intrinsic part of our nature (or of the natural man) to do so: "It is the constitutional disposition of mankind to set up stakes and set bounds to the works and ways of the Almighty."[12] "Many," he said, "seal up the door of heaven by saying so far God may reveal and I will believe" but no further.[13] He commented that even Latter-day Saints were unprepared to hear all the truth: "If the Church knew all the commandments, one half they would condemn through prejudice and ignorance."[14] President Joseph Fielding Smith made a similar observation: "If the Lord should reveal to us all that he taught Enoch and other prophets, there would be many members of the Church who would rebel and turn away in opposition to it."[15]

Joseph counseled the Saints about the attitude they need to have if they are to receive all the Lord, in His generosity, desires to give to us: "There are those who profess to be Saints who are too apt to murmur, and find fault, when any advice is given, which comes in opposition to their feelings, even when they, themselves, ask for counsel; much more so when counsel is given unasked for, which does not agree with their notion of things; but brethren, we hope for better things from the most of you; we trust that you desire counsel, from time to time, and that you will cheerfully conform to it, whenever you receive it from a proper source."[16]

Joseph also lamented that the "Saints were slow to understand," and he compared the difficulty of getting "anything into the heads of this generation" to "trying to split a hemlock knot with a corn dodger [a piece of corn bread] for a wedge and a pumpkin for a beetle [hammer]." He added, "I have tried for a number of years to get the minds of the Saints prepared to receive the things of God, but we frequently see some of them after suffering all they have for the work of God will fly to peaces like glass as soon as any thing comes that is contrary to their traditions, they cannot stand the fire at all."[17]

While in Nauvoo, "the Apostles and a few others met at the Prophet's home on a Sunday evening. . . . Joseph followed [one of the speakers] with an acknowledgment that some dissatisfaction existed in Nauvoo because he did not deliver to the Saints more of the word of God. The Saints, he said in defense, were not prepared to receive what he had, "No (says he) not one in this room." He then chastised those present for unbelief and further explained that one reason the Saints did not have the secrets of the Lord was their inability to maintain confidences. "I can keep a secret till doomsday," he added.[18]

The Saints were simply not always prepared to receive all that Joseph had to impart. He had more to offer than they were able to receive. Speaking of the vision of the degrees of glory in the Resurrection (D&C 76), the Prophet said, "I could explain a hundred fold more than I ever have of the glories of the kingdoms manifested to me in the vision, were I permitted, and were the people prepared to receive them."[19]

Yet he held out hope that they would come to see the light: "God hath not revealed anything to Joseph, but what He will make known unto the Twelve, and even the least Saint may know all things as fast as he is able to bear them."[20] Joseph held out mercy for those who were trying to learn. He said, "It does not prove that a man is not a good man because he errs in doctrine."[21]

God is willing to give away the secrets of the universe, the origins of life, and the purpose for our existence, if we will just open our hearts and minds to receive them. They have been revealed to modern prophets, and each of us can go to the exact same source and receive our own witness from the Holy Ghost that what the prophets have taught and testified is true (Moroni 10:3–5).

There are many evidences for the certainty of the Restoration. The following chapters identify six of the most important.

Notes

1. As cited in Hyrum L. Andrus, *Little Known Friends of the Prophet Joseph Smith* (Salt Lake City: Deseret Book, 1998), 5.

2. As cited in Truman G. Madsen, *Joseph Smith the Prophet* (Salt Lake City: Bookcraft, 1989), 144–45.

3. Brigham Young, in *Journal of Discourses*, 26 vols. (London: Latter-day Saints' Book Depot, 1854–86), 12:270.

4. Ibid., 4:54.

5. Wandle Mace, *Writings of Early Latter-day Saints and Their Contemporaries, a Database Collection*, comp. Milton V. Backman (Provo, Utah: BYU Religious Studies Center, 1996), 164.

6. Joseph Smith, *Teachings of the Prophet Joseph Smith*, comp. Joseph Fielding Smith (Salt Lake City: Deseret Book, 1976), 256.

7. Joseph Smith, in *Journal of Discourses*, 6:4.

8. *The Words of Joseph Smith*, comp. and ed. Andrew F. Ehat and Lyndon W. Cook (Orem, Utah: Grandin Book, 1991), 358.

9. Smith, *History of the Church*, 276.

10. Smith, *Teachings*, 51.

11. Ibid., 321.

12. Ibid., 320.

13. As cited in *The Prophet Joseph: Essays on the Life and Mission of Joseph Smith*, ed. Larry C. Porter and Susan Easton Black (Salt Lake City: Deseret Book, 1988), 317; compare this with his letter from Liberty Jail to Isaac Galland, 22 March 1839: "Where is the man who is authorized to put his finger on the spot and say, thus far thou shalt go and no farther: there is no man. Therefore let us receive the whole, or none" (*Times and Seasons* [February 1840]: 55).

14. Smith, *History of the Church*, 2:477.

15. Joseph Fielding Smith, *Signs of the Times* (Salt Lake City: Deseret Book, 1952) 8–9.

16. Smiht, *History of the Church*, 4:45.

17. As cited in Ronald K. Esplin, "Joseph, Brigham, and the Twelve: a Succession of Continuity," *BYU Studies* (Summer 1981): 303.

18. Ibid., 312–13.

19. Smith, *History of the Church*, 5:402.

20. Smith, *Teachings*, 149.

21. Joseph Smith, general conference address, Nauvoo, 8 April 1843; as cited in Smith, *History of the Church*, 5:340.

CHAPTER SIX

FIRST EVIDENCE FOR THE REALITY OF THE RESTORATION:

Others, Besides Joseph Smith, Received Spiritual Confirmations and Personal Witnesses from the Spirit

Mesmerizing speakers can move audiences to tears. Feelings can be manipulated. But personal spiritual experiences and visitations from divine beings carry their own testimony of the truth. Those who associated with the Prophet Joseph Smith recorded numerous personal spiritual experiences and confirmations of the Restoration. Several of them later fell away from the Church, or became disaffected from their friendship with the Prophet, but even these individuals continued to bear witness of what they, themselves, had seen and heard. Spiritual experiences of this nature simply cannot be faked or forced upon others, and the fact that those who joined the Church received them is one of the first evidences for the reality of the Restoration.

The Book of Mormon itself closes with the promise that every person is entitled to their own witness of its truthfulness and promises that "by the power of the Holy Ghost, ye may know the truth of all things" (Moroni 10:5).

What is it that first plants the desire in people's hearts to want to know the truth for themselves? The Prophet Joseph answered, "Human testimony and human testimony only . . . excite[s] this inquiry, in the first instance, in their minds."[1] When people first heard the message of the Restoration and Joseph Smith's testimony of his own experiences, they wanted to know the truth for themselves. They were not disappointed. Many who heard Joseph teach received personal testimonies of the truth. One British convert, James Palmer, said: "[He] looked and had the appearance of one that was heaven born while preaching or as tho [sic] he had been sent from the heavenly worlds on a divine mission." Another convert, Wandle Mace, added, "Joseph has been feeding us deliciously with spiritual food."[2]

President Brigham Young noted that "those who were acquainted with him knew when the Spirit of revelation was on him, for his countenance wore an expression peculiar to himself while under that influence. He preached by the Spirit of revelation, and taught in his council by it, and those who were acquainted with him could discover it at once, for at such times there was a peculiar clearness and transparency in his face."[3] President Wilford Woodruff added, "He seemed a fountain of knowledge from whose mouth streams of eternal wisdom flowed; and as he stood before the people, he showed that the authority of God was upon him."[4]

We have several accounts written by individuals who witnessed the Spirit as it rested on the Prophet Joseph Smith. Emmeline Blanch Wells said:

> It seems to me I could fill pages upon pages describing my own thought of this magnificent personage, and with what I have heard from those who knew him, so much better and more intimately. But this I will say in closing this imperfectly written reminiscence. He was beyond my comprehension. The power of God rested upon him to such a degree that on many occasions he seemed transfigured. His expression was mild and almost childlike

in repose; and when addressing the people, . . . the glory of his countenance was beyond description. At other times the great power of his manner, more than of his voice (which was sublimely eloquent to me) seemed to shake the place on which we stood and penetrate the inmost soul of his hearers, and I am sure that then they would have laid down their lives to defend him. I always listened spellbound to his every utterance—the chosen of God in this last dispensation.[5]

Mary Elizabeth Rollins Lightner recorded meeting Joseph Smith in Kirtland, Ohio, and attending a gathering where she heard him speak. She shared this remarkable experience:

I joined the Church in the year 1830, in Kirtland, Ohio, just six months after it was first organized. I was then twelve years old.

The Smith family came to Kirtland early in the spring of 1831. After they were settled in their house, mother and I went to see them. We had heard so much about the Golden Bible, as it was then called, that we were very anxious to hear more. The whole Smith family, excepting Joseph, was there. As we stood talking to them, Brother Joseph and Martin Harris came in with two or three others. When the greetings were over, Brother Joseph looked around very solemnly (it was the first time some of them had ever seen him) and said, "There are enough here to hold a little meeting."

A board was put across two chairs to make seats. Martin Harris sat on a little box at Joseph's feet. They sang and prayed, then

Joseph got up to speak. He began very solemnly and very earnestly; all at once his countenance changed and he stood mute. He turned so white, he seemed perfectly transparent. Those who looked at him that night said he looked like he had a searchlight within him. I never saw anything like it on earth. I could not take my eyes away from him. I remember I thought we could almost see the bones through the flesh of his face.

I shall remember his as he looked then as long as I live.

He stood some moments looking over the congregation, as if to pierce each heart, then said, "Do you know who has been in your midst this night?"

One of the Smiths said, "An angel of the Lord."

Martin Harris said, "It was our Lord and Savior, Jesus Christ."

Joseph put his hand down on Martin's head and said,

"The Spirit of God revealed that to thee. Yes, brothers and sisters, the Savior has been in your midst this night, and I want you all to remember it. There is a veil over your eyes, for you could not endure to look upon him. You must be fed with milk not with strong meat. I want you all to remember this as if it were the last thing that escapes my lips."[6]

Mary Ann Winters was present at a meeting in Nauvoo when Joseph spoke to a group of Native Americans: "I stood close by the Prophet while he was preaching to the Indians in the Grove by the Temple. The Holy Spirit lighted up his countenance till it glowed like a halo around him, and his words penetrated the hearts of all who heard him and the Indians looked as solemn as eternity."[7]

Others, like William Henrie, felt the Spirit when Joseph preached: "You could not be in [the Prophet's] presence without feeling the influence and Spirit of God, which seemed to flow from him almost as heat does from a stove. You could not see it, but you felt it."[8]

Still others not only felt the Spirit but were also privileged to see God, the Savior, and angels. Joseph was rarely alone when he beheld heavenly visions. The first time the Prophet saw the Father and the Son he was alone in the Sacred Grove. But there are at least four other incidents where the Father and the Son appeared to the Prophet Joseph, and on each of these four occasions there were others with him who also saw what he did.[9] Spiritual experiences such as these simply cannot be manufactured out of thin air, nor were they ever denied by those who experienced them.

Oliver Cowdery was present when John the Baptist and, later, Peter, James and John the Revelator appeared and laid their hands on Joseph Smith's and Oliver Cowdery's heads to confer upon them the priesthood. Although he left the Church for almost a decade, he never denied his experiences of seeing the angels who appeared to him. When he returned and rejoined the Church, he bore fervent testimony of what he knew to be true: "I was present with Joseph when an holy angel from god came down from heaven and conferred or restored the Aaronic priesthood. And said at the same time that it should remain upon the earth while the earth stands. I was also present with Joseph when the Melchizedek priesthood was conferred by the holy angels of god."[10]

The Three Witnesses to the Book of Mormon (Oliver Cowdery, David Whitmer, and Martin Harris) continually affirmed that they had indeed seen the angel Moroni who showed them the Book of Mormon plates. Edward

Stevenson said of Oliver Cowdery, "I have often heard him bear a faithful testimony to the restoration of the gospel by the visitation of an angel, in whose presence he stood in company with the Prophet Joseph Smith and David Whitmer. He testified that he beheld the plates, the leaves being turned over by the angel, whose voice he heard, and that they were commanded as witnesses to bear a faithful testimony to the world of the vision that they were favored to behold, and that the translation from the plates of the Book of Mormon was accepted of the Lord, and that it would go forth to the world, and that no power on the earth should stop its progress."

Stevenson said that in 1886 he heard David Whitmer bear a similar witness. Whitmer had left the Church almost forty years earlier yet testified: "As sure as the sun shines and I live, just so sure did the angel appear to me and Joseph Smith, and I heard his voice, and did see the angel standing before us, and on a table were the plates, the sword of Laban and the ball [Liahona] or compass." Stevenson said that while on a mission he visited Kirtland and met Martin Harris (the other of the Three Witnesses to the Book of Mormon) who bore the same testimony.[11]

Thomas B. Marsh met David Whitmer and Oliver Cowdery after they had both apostatized from the Church. He said, "I enquired seriously of David if it was true that he had seen the angel, according to his testimony as one of the witnesses of the Book of Mormon. He replied as sure as there is a God in heaven, he saw the angel according to his testimony in that book. I asked him, if so, why he did not stand by Joseph? He answered, in the days when Joseph received the Book of Mormon, and brought it forth, he was a good man and filled with the Holy Ghost, but he considered he had now fallen. I interrogated Oliver Cowdery in the same manner, who answered similarly."[12]

Thus, the preponderance of additional witnesses to the truth becomes one of the first evidences for the reality of the Restoration. Many others saw and knew for themselves that what Joseph Smith had taught was true. Today, millions more all across the earth in practically every nation and among all cultures—all independent of one another—bear testimony that they have also received spiritual confirmations that the Church is true and that the gospel of Jesus Christ has indeed been restored. As the Apostle Paul testified, "In the mouth of two or three witnesses shall every word be established" (2 Corinthians 13:1). What then shall we think of an event (the Restoration) that today has millions of people who bear witness of its truthfulness?

Notes

1. Joseph Smith, *Lectures on Faith* (Salt Lake City: Deseret Book, 1985), 24.

2. As cited in *Church History in the Fulness of Times*, Institute Student Manual, prepared by the Church Educational System (Salt Lake City: The Church of Jesus Christ of Latter-day Saints, 1989), 259.

3. Brigham Young, in *Journal of Discourses*, 26 vols. (London: Latter-day Saints' Book Depot, 1854–86), 9:89.

4. Wilford Woodruff, *Journal History* (L. Tom Perry Special Collections, Harold B. Lee Library, Brigham Young University, Provo, Utah), 9 April 1837.

5. "Joseph Smith, the Prophet," *Young Woman's Journal* (1905): 556.

6. Ibid., 556–57.

7. Ibid., 558.

8. As cited in *Remembering Joseph*, comp. Mark L. McConkie (Salt Lake City: Deseret Book, 2003), 358.

9. Visitations of the Father and the Son: Sacred Grove (Joseph Smith–History 1:17); general conference, June 1831, at the Issac Morely Farm, Kirtland, Ohio (*Levi Hancock Journal* (BYU Special Collections), 33, and *Journal History* 1:56–57; in John Johnson's

home at Hiram, Ohio (D&C 76:20, 23); in the School of the Prophets, Newel K. Whitney store in Kirtland (*History of the Church*, 1:334–35); in the Kirtland Temple (D&C 137:1–3).

10. As recorded in *Reuben Miller Journal* (21 October 1848): 14. Report of "Conference held on Misqueto Creek, Council Bluffs October 21st 1848"; as cited in "Priesthood Restoration Documents," *BYU Studies* 35 (1996): 184.

11. Andrew Jenson, *Latter-day Saint Biographical Encyclopedia: A Compilation of Biographical Sketches of Prominent Men and Women in The Church of Jesus Christ of Latter-day Saints*, 4 vols. (Salt Lake City: The Andrew Jenson History Co., 1901), 1:215.

12. *Millennial Star* 26 (1864): 406.

CHAPTER SEVEN

SECOND EVIDENCE FOR THE
REALITY OF THE RESTORATION:

The Prophet Joseph Smith's Mission Was Foreknown and Foretold

Many ancient prophets foresaw Joseph Smith's life and work. The Restoration was one of the great themes upon which former-day prophets dwelt with delight, and it is not surprising to find prophetic statements regarding Joseph Smith. Here are a few of the more significant statements from ancient prophets.

Joseph who was sold into Egypt. One of the marvelous prophecies of the Restoration was uttered by the ancient patriarch Joseph (JST Genesis 50, JST Appendix). He was shown that a descendant of his—a "choice seer"—would be raised up in the latter-days (2 Nephi 3:6–7). This seer would be "esteemed highly," his work would be of great worth, and he would gather Israel like Moses (2 Nephi 3:7–9). Joseph of Egypt said this latter-day seer would bring forth a record (the Book of Mormon) that would bear witness to the world that the scriptures already sent forth by the Lord (the Bible) were true (2 Nephi 3:11–12; see also 1 Nephi 13:35–36, 39–41). Joseph of Egypt saw that these two records would "grow together" and confound false doctrine, establish peace, and bring people to a knowledge of the ancient prophets and to a knowledge of the Lord's covenants (2 Nephi 3:12; compare Ezekiel 37:15–17). Joseph of Egypt also prophesied that "out of weakness, he [the choice seer] shall be made strong" (2 Nephi 3:13). Perhaps one of Joseph of Egypt's most precise prophecies about Joseph Smith is that his name would be Joseph, like his father's (2 Nephi 3:15). With three older brothers, it was a miracle that Joseph Smith was the son who received his father's name, but just as foreknown, it occurred.

Moses. The great lawgiver, Moses, was also made aware of Joseph Smith's role in restoring precious and plain scriptures that would be lost from the Bible. Moses was shown a vision of the creation and was commanded to write it. Moses was told what would happen to the words he would write and was also informed of Joseph Smith's mission to restore them: "And now Moses, my son, I will speak unto thee concerning this earth upon which thou standest; and thou shalt write the things which I shall speak. And in the day when the children of men shall esteem my words as naught and take many of them from the book which thou shalt write, behold I will raise up another like unto thee and they shall be had again among the children of men, among as many as shall believe" (Moses 1:40–41).

Joseph Smith was the prophet raised up who restored the words of Moses to the biblical record. (Compare Genesis 1:1–6:13 with Moses 1–8 to see a portion of what Joseph restored.)

Isaiah. The prophet Isaiah also foresaw Joseph Smith's work and even recorded conversations Joseph Smith's associates would have regarding the translation of the Book of Mormon. (Compare Isaiah 29:11–14 with Joseph Smith–History 1:63–65). The entire prophecy in Isaiah 29 has reference to the coming forth of the Book of Mormon. (Compare Isaiah 29 with 2 Nephi 27.)

Malachi. The prophet Malachi foresaw a latter-day forerunner who would build temples to prepare the world for the Second Coming (Malachi 3:1). On August 3, 1831 (when the Church had been organized for only sixteen months), Joseph Smith dedicated the cornerstones for the first temple at Independence, Missouri.[1] On March 27, 1836, he dedicated the Kirtland Temple (D&C 109). It was in this temple one week later, on April 3, 1836 (Passover), that Joseph Smith met and received divine authority from the Savior, Moses, Elias, and Elijah (D&C 110). Elijah's appearance in the Kirtland Temple on the day of Passover signaled the fulfillment of another prophecy of Malachi (Malachi 4:5–6; D&C 110:13–16).

Joseph also designed and built the Nauvoo Temple and had a site for a temple dedicated at Far West, Missouri, but the Saints were prevented by mobocracy from building this temple (D&C 124:47–51).

Besides building temples, the Prophet Joseph also revealed the purpose of temples and restored specific temple ordinances to be performed in them for both the living and in behalf of our deceased ancestors. Today, as a result of Joseph Smith's temple-building initiative and because of succeeding prophets' efforts (especially those of President Gordon B. Hinckley) there are over 120 temples in operation or under construction. Nothing else in the history of modern Christianity compares to how Malachi's prophecies were fulfilled by the Prophet Joseph Smith and the Latter-day Saints.

The Savior to the Nephites. In 3 Nephi 21, the Savior described to the ancient Nephites how Joseph Smith would bring forth the Book of Mormon—the sign that the gathering of Israel had begun—and launch the Restoration (3 Nephi 21:1–9). The Savior described how Joseph's life would be safeguarded until his mission was completed: "The life of my servant shall be in my hand; therefore they shall not hurt him, although he shall be marred because of them. Yet I will heal him" (3 Nephi 21:10).

Joseph was marred. In 1832, he was tarred and feathered by a mob and left for dead. "My friends," he said, "spent the night in scraping and removing the tar, and washing and cleansing my body." The next morning was the Sabbath and with great faith and effort, Joseph greeted a group, among whom were some of the mobbers from the night before. "With my flesh all scarified and defaced, I preached to the congregation as usual, and in the afternoon of the same day baptized three individuals."[2] These baptisms were performed in a nearby stream, which had to have the ice chopped away to reach the water.

A few months later while traveling through Indiana, Joseph and those accompanying him had to leap from a runaway stagecoach. Bishop Newel K. Whitney slipped, breaking his leg in several places. Joseph stayed with Bishop Whitney for weeks, caring for him. One night their dinner was poisoned. As a result, Joseph vomited so violently that he dislocated his jaw. He had to reset it himself. Bishop Whitney administered to him, and Joseph was healed immediately, although the effects of the poison caused him to lose some of his hair.[3] He was "marred," but Joseph was preserved by the Lord to finish the Lord's work.

Even the Book of Mormon was "marred" when the 116 pages of the book of Lehi were lost through carelessness to traitors (D&C 3 and 10). But the Lord had known of this loss for centuries before it occurred, and with His divine foresight inspired prophets to prepare the record in such a way so that the lost 116 page manuscript would not cripple the completed text (Words of Mormon 1:5–7; D&C 10:38–45). Thus, the Book of Mormon was marred, but it too was healed by the Lord to accomplish His purposes.

Peter, James, and John. Peter, James, and John also knew about the Prophet Joseph Smith. While returning from the Mount of Transfiguration, the Savior told them about one who was to "come and restore all things, as it is written by the prophets" (JST Matthew 17:10-11). They assumed he was referring to John the Baptist. But as the Savior explained further, they "understood that he spake unto them of John the Baptist *and also of another who should come and restore all things* as it is written by the prophets" (JST Appendix, Matthew 17:14).

Joseph Smith is this other prophet to whom Peter, James, and John themselves appeared in 1829 to restore the authority and keys of the Melchizedek Priesthood, which they held. President Wilford Woodruff declared, "The Lord chose Joseph Smith to establish this Church and kingdom. He brought forth the blessings of the Gospel. He received the holy Priesthood from the angels of God."[4]

Peter also prophesied about the First Vision—the appearance of the Father and the Son to Joseph Smith—which began "the restitution of all things" (Acts 3:19-21).

The Savior to His Disciples. Even the Savior, while delivering His final discourse on the Mount of Olives about His second coming and the latter days, indicated something about Joseph's role as the primary witness to the world regarding the Restoration: "This Gospel of the Kingdom shall be preached in all the world, for a witness unto all nations, and then shall the end come, or the destruction of the wicked" (Joseph Smith–Matthew 1:31).

In an address to the Saints in Nauvoo in May 1844, just weeks before he was slain, the Prophet Joseph translated this same verse from his German Bible and rendered it a little differently. The Germans who were present said he translated it correctly: "And it will be preached, the Gospel of the kingdom, to the whole world, *to a witness* over all people; and then will the end come." The Prophet Joseph then offered an inspired commentary, noting his role in the unfolding drama of this last dispensation: "The Savior said when these tribulations should take place, it [the gospel of the kingdom] should be committed to *a man who should be a witness over the whole world:* the keys of knowledge, power and revelations should be revealed to *a witness* who should hold the testimony to the world. . . . All the testimony is that the Lord in the last days would commit the keys of the priesthood *to a witness* over all people."[5]

Who is this witness, this prophesied messenger, who would receive the gospel of Jesus Christ from angels, and who would then declare this testimony to the whole world? This prophesied messenger of the covenant is decidedly the Prophet Joseph Smith. Lorenzo Snow reported hearing several individuals ask Joseph Smith who he was. On one occasion the Prophet replied to his questioner, "Noah came before the flood. I have come before the fire."[6]

John the Baptist. John the Baptist knew of and prophesied of Joseph Smith. When the priests and Levites asked John who he was, "he confessed and denied not that he was Elias [the forerunner]; but confessed, saying; I am not the Christ. And they asked him, saying; How then art thou Elias? And he said, *I am not that Elias who was to restore all things.* And they asked him, saying, *art thou that prophet?* And he answered, No" (JST Appendix, John 1:20–22). Joseph Smith is the modern Elias spoken of by John the Baptist, to whom John the Baptist appeared on May 15, 1829 (D&C 13).

President John Taylor offered another testimony that many prophets had a knowledge of him centuries before he was born:

> Joseph Smith in the first place was set apart
> by the Almighty according to the counsels of
> the gods in the eternal worlds, to introduce the
> principles of life among the people, of which

the Gospel is the grand power and influence, and through which salvation can extend to all peoples, all nations, all kindreds, all tongues and all worlds. It is the principle that brings life and immortality to light, and places us in communication with God. God selected him for that purpose, and he fulfilled his mission and lived honorably and died honorably.[7]

If Joseph Smith is not the latter-day prophet of whom these ancient prophets spoke, then we must look for another. Who else could it possibly be? Joseph Smith's fulfillment of ancient prophecies was not sporadic or happenstance. There were numerous, highly specific, prophetic utterances that his life and mission fulfilled. Unlike most preachers of the Bible, Joseph did not merely cite scripture to teach gospel principles, he also testified that he and the work the Lord was doing through him was a direct fulfillment of those prophecies. The Prophet Joseph's mission was foreknown by ancient prophets. It seems as though they were very aware of Joseph's latter-day mission.

JOSEPH'S PERSONAL ACQUAINTANCE WITH ANCIENT PROPHETS

Not only did the ancient prophets know of Joseph Smith and prophesy of his mission, but Joseph also knew them—personally and intimately. To those who believe in the ministry of angels, the Book of Mormon declares:

Has the day of miracles ceased? Or have angels ceased to appear unto the children of men? Or has he withheld the power of the Holy Ghost from them? Or will he, so long as time shall last, or the earth shall stand, or there shall be one man upon the face thereof to be saved?

Behold I say unto you, Nay; for it is by faith that miracles are wrought; and it is by faith that angels appear and minister unto men; wherefore, if these things have ceased wo be unto the children of men, for it is because of unbelief . . .

. . . . For behold, God knowing all things, being from everlasting to everlasting, behold, he sent angels to minister unto the children of men, to make manifest concerning the coming of Christ; and in Christ there should come every good thing.

And God also declared unto prophets, by his own mouth, that Christ should come. (Moroni 7:35–37, 22–23)

In the spring of 1820, Joseph Smith was visited not only by the Father and the Son but also by "many angels."[8] The heavens opened again in 1823 when Moroni appeared, followed in subsequent years by a host of other heavenly messengers all declaring their dispensations, their rights, their privileges, and their keys of authority (Joseph Smith–History 1:27–54; D&C 128:20-21).[9] In preparation for translating the Book of Mormon, the angel Moroni showed Joseph Smith in vision the ancient inhabitants of the Americas. His mother said, "During our evening conversations, Joseph would . . . describe the ancient inhabitants of [the American] continent, their dress, mode of traveling, and the animals upon which they rode; their cities, their buildings, with every particular; their mode of warfare; and also their religious worship. This he would do with as much ease, seemingly, as if he had spent his whole life among them."[10]

John Taylor further noted Joseph Smith's familiarity with ancient prophets:

> I know of what I speak, for I was very well acquainted with him and was with him a great deal during his life, and was with him when he died. The principles which he had, placed him in communication with the Lord, and not only with the Lord, but with the ancient apostles and prophets; such men, for instance, as Abraham, Isaac, Jacob, Noah, Adam, Seth, Enoch, and Jesus and the Father, and the apostles that lived on this continent as well as those who lived on the Asiatic continent. He seemed to be as familiar with these people as we are with one another. Why? Because he had to introduce a dispensation which was called the dispensation of the fullness of times, and it was known as such by the ancient servants of God.[11]

"Who among the world scholars," Joseph Fielding McConkie observed, "can boast of having stood face to face with Adam, Enoch, Noah, a messenger from Abraham's dispensation, Moses, John [the Baptist], Peter, James, and John? While religious leaders were claiming that the heavens were sealed to them, Joseph Smith was being personally tutored by ancient prophets who laid their hands upon his head and conferred upon him the power, keys, and authority they held. . . . Who but Joseph Smith could tell us that Seth was in the perfect likeness of his father (see D&C 107:43), or could give a detailed description of Paul? (see *Teachings of the Prophet Joseph Smith*, 180)"[12] or describe personal visits with John the Beloved?[13]

Hyrum Smith left this testimony of his brother's calling

as a prophet of God: "There were prophets before, but Joseph has the spirit and power of all the prophets."[14] Joseph knew the Bible, he knew its authors, and they knew him.

Notes

1. Joseph Smith, *History of The Church of Jesus Christ of Latter-day Saints*, ed. B. H. Roberts, 2d ed. rev., 7 vols. (Salt Lake City: The Church of Jesus Christ of Latter-day Saints, 1980), 1:199.

2. Ibid., 1:264.

3. Ibid., 1:271.

4. *Collected Discourses*, 5 vols., comp. Brian H. Stuy (Burbank: B.H.S. Publishing, 1987–92), 1:312.

5. Joseph Smith, *Teachings of the Prophet Joseph Smith*, comp. Joseph Fielding Smith (Salt Lake City: Deseret Book, 1976), 364.

6. As cited in Truman G. Madsen, *Joseph Smith the Prophet* (Salt Lake City: Bookcraft, 1989), 105.

7. John Taylor, in *Journal of Discourses*, 26 vols. (London: Latter-day Saints' Book Depot, 1854–86), 21:94.

8. Milton V. Backman Jr., "Joseph Smith's Recitals of the First Vision," *Ensign*, January 1985, 14.

9. Many testified of the divine messengers who appeared to Joseph, as recorded in the *Journal of Discourses* (Orson Pratt, 13:66; 15:185; John Taylor, 21:94; 17:374–75; 21:161–64; Wilford Woodruff, 16:34–35.

10. Lucy Mack Smith, *History of Joseph Smith by His Mother Lucy Mack Smith* (Salt Lake City: Bookcraft, 1958), 83.

11. John Taylor, in *Journal of Discourses*, 21:94.

12. Joseph F. McConkie, "Joseph Smith and the Poetic Writings," *The Joseph Smith Translation: The Restoration of Plain and Precious Things*, ed. Monte S. Nyman and Robert L. Millet (Provo, Utah: BYU Religious Studies Center, 1985), 118–19.

13. Oliver Boardman Huntington, *Diary of Oliver Boardman Huntington 1847–1900*, part 2 (L. Tom Perry Special Collections, Harold B. Lee Library, Brigham Young University, Provo, Utah), 162.

14. Smith, *History of the Church*, 6:346.

CHAPTER EIGHT

THIRD EVIDENCE FOR THE REALITY OF THE RESTORATION:

The Events of the Restoration Were Foreseen by Ancient Prophets

Prophets are both forth-tellers who call us to repentance and fore-tellers (seers) who are shown the future (Mosiah 8:16–18). Recorded in the scriptures are numerous prophecies of future occurrences, which were revealed to ancient prophets. Many of these are focused on the events of the latter days. Thus, the events of the Restoration were foreknown and foreseen by ancient Biblical prophets. As mentioned, Joseph Smith said, "It is a theme upon which prophets, priests and kings have dwelt with peculiar delight."[1] The fact that all the major events of the Restoration were previously described in some detail in the scriptures is another evidence that the Restoration came from the Lord through the Prophet Joseph.

Ancient prophets described that a time of "refreshing [would] come from the presence of the Lord" when the Father and the Son would appear to begin the restitution of all things all the former prophets had received (Acts 3:19–21) and that angels would participate in the restoration of these truths (Revelation 14:6–7).

Other prophets (including Isaiah, Ezekiel, King David, Nephi, and Enoch) foresaw that in the last days preceding the Second Coming, a book would come forth out of the earth to stand as a second witness to the truthfulness of

the Bible and to bear testimony that Jesus Christ had resurrected from the dead and is the Redeemer of all mankind (Psalm 85; Ezekiel 37:15–17; Isaiah 29; Moses 7:62;
1 Nephi 13:39–40).

Others taught of the importance of having the proper
authority from God to administer the ordinances of salvation and to build up the Church (Ephesians 4:11–14). They
prophesied that God would raise up and send one vested
with this authority to restore all things (JST John 1:20–22;
Acts 3:20-21).

Prophets also taught that specific offices were established in the Church in the beginning and that a church,
in order to belong to the Savior, must have these same
offices and bear the name of Jesus Christ (Ephesians 4:11;
3 Nephi 27:7–10). "How be it my church," the Savior asked
the Nephites and Lamanites in ancient America, "save it be
called in my name?" (3 Nephi 27:8).

Ancient prophets foretold a time when, in the latter days,
God would gather scattered Israel back to the covenant and
eventually to their covenant lands (Isaiah 5:16; Jeremiah
16:14-21; Ezekiel 37; Amos 9:11-15; Zechariah 10:6-12;
1 Nephi 22:8-12, 25; 3 Nephi 20:29-41; 21).

For the past two millennia, since the time when the
Savior walked and taught on earth, there has only been one
individual to step out and claim the fulfillment of all these
ancient prophecies. Joseph Smith told of being divinely
guided to find and translate a book that came out of the
earth, written by the ancient inhabitants of the Americas,
which bears witness of the resurrected Christ and described
His magnificent appearance in ancient America.

Joseph testified that the Father and the Son appeared
to him in the spring of 1820 and called him to restore the
Church of Jesus Christ to the earth with all its officers and
organization. Joseph bore witness that all those who held

priesthood keys and authority in ancient times appeared to him and by the laying on of hands committed that same priesthood to him. Joseph was inspired to restore the ordinances of baptism and imparting the gift of the Holy Ghost so that those who receive it experience the prophesied gifts of the Spirit.

If Joseph Smith is not to be believed, then we would have to look for another to fulfill all these ancient prophecies. Where else would we find such a restorer?

OTHER PROPHECIES FULFILLED

The Prophet Joseph fulfilled all these, and many other prophecies, during his lifetime. For example, Nephi foresaw the rapid growth of The Church of Jesus Christ of Latter-day Saints: "I beheld that the church of the Lamb of God, and its numbers were few. . . . nevertheless, I beheld that the Church of the Lamb, who were the saints of God, were also upon all the face of the earth" (1 Nephi 14:12). This prophecy has been and yet continues to be fulfilled in miraculous ways.

The Old Testament prophet Jeremiah foresaw the westward trek of the Saints to the Rocky Mountains and Brigham Young's colonizing efforts. Jeremiah (and others) knew the Saints would be organized "in the height of Zion," in the tops of the "everlasting hills" where the headquarters of the Church stands today (Jeremiah 31:12; 30:20–22, 24; 31:6–14; Genesis 49:26; 1 Nephi 13:37).

Micah and Isaiah also saw the Saints headquartered in the tops of the everlasting mountains. There they would establish the "mountain of the Lord's house"—the beautiful Salt Lake Temple and the incomparable LDS Conference Center—to which "all nations shall flow" to learn of God's ways so they can "walk in his paths" (Micah 4:1-2; Isaiah 2:2-3). The LDS Conference Center even resembles a mountain—made of large granite blocks, with trees planted along the walls, including a six-acre park on the roof and a river cascading over the roof and down the front wall. It is literally "the mountain of the Lord's house." And thanks to the miracle of modern satellite technology, the word of the Lord can be broadcast from the "mountain of the Lord's house" located in the "tops of the mountains" to the ends of the earth in scores of languages simultaneously.[2]

Jeremiah foresaw the modern missionary force and the miraculous latter-day gathering of Israel. "Hunter" and "fisher" missionaries, as Jeremiah described them, are being sent out by the tens of thousands to seek out the righteous wherever they may be (Jeremiah 16:14–16). "Hunters" are bringing converts "one of a city, and two of a family" (Jeremiah 3:14), while "fishers" are gathering entire groups of people into the gospel net. The gathering of Israel in these latter days truly is a "marvelous work and a wonder" (2 Nephi 25:17).

Daniel foresaw a stone cut out without hands that would roll forth and fill the whole earth (Daniel 2:34-35). In 1831, the Lord identified his latter-day Church as that stone (D&C 65). Daniel said it would "never be destroyed" and that it would "stand forever" (Daniel 2:44.) Commenting on these verses, Joseph Smith said, "I calculate to be one of the instruments of setting up the kingdom of Daniel by the word of the Lord, and I intend to lay a foundation that will revolutionize the whole world. . . . It will not be by sword or gun that this kingdom will roll on: the power of truth is such that all nations will be under the necessity of obeying the Gospel."[3] President Heber J. Grant testified that The Church of Jesus Christ of Latter-day Saints is the fulfillment of Daniel's prophecy: "I bear my witness to you here today that Joseph Smith was a prophet of the true and living God, that he was the instrument in the hands of God of establishing again upon the earth the plan of life and salvation, not only for the living but for the dead, and that this gospel, commonly called 'Mormonism,' by the people of the world, is in very deed the plan of life and salvation, the gospel of the Lord Jesus Christ, and that the little stone has been cut out of the mountain, and that it shall roll forth until it fills the whole earth."[4] President Gordon B. Hinckley has similarly noted that the Church will continue to go forward: "This cause will roll on in majesty and power to fill the earth. Doors now closed to the preaching of the gospel will be opened. The Almighty, if necessary, may have to shake the nations to humble them and cause them to listen to the servants of the living God. Whatever is needed will come to pass."[5]

People may be surprised that there are so many scriptural evidences existing in the Bible concerning the Restoration, which were fulfilled by Joseph Smith. Joseph Smith and Oliver Cowdery were themselves surprised at the great amount of evidence in the Bible concerning the things they were experiencing and receiving.[6] All who study the doctrine they introduced can go to the Bible and find evidences for it. There they will find that what Joseph Smith did and taught under the inspiration of the Spirit is in perfect harmony with the doctrines taught by inspired men of God in ancient times. The breadth and beauty of these doctrines penetrate the soul, and all opinions and man-made creeds sink into insignificance when compared with the message that came directly from heaven. Elder Orson Pratt declared, "No one ever will be able to confute their [the Latter-day Saints'] doctrine by the scriptures; however imperfect the people may be, their doctrine is infallible."[7] It fits perfectly all that has been revealed in the past because it came from heaven. Joseph received revelation from the same source as the ancient apostles and prophets.

If it were not for revelation from heaven, the people called the Latter-day Saints would not be in existence. Without revelation there would be no organization of The Church of Jesus Christ of Latter-day Saints. Without revelation there would be no missionary message and no missionaries called to travel to the ends of the earth to bear testimony of the truths of the everlasting gospel. The rock upon which this Church is built, and the solid foundation upon which it has grown, is divine revelation from God—the very rock the Savior told Peter His church was originally founded upon (Matthew 16:16–19). That is why the doctrines taught in the Church and organization of this Church are all in perfect harmony with the truths taught in the Bible. As Elder George Q. Cannon testified, "It made no difference to Joseph Smith whether he read and was familiar with every doctrine taught by the Apostles; he was under no necessity of framing his teachings therewith that there should be no difference between that which he taught, and that which had been taught, because the same spirit that revealed to the ancient Apostles and Prophets, and inspired them to teach the people . . . taught him also and enabled him to teach exactly the same truths."[8]

1845 PROCLAMATION OF THE TWELVE

As mentioned previously, the Twelve Apostles, not many months after the martyrdom of the Prophet Joseph Smith, issued a stirring proclamation to the world in which they reminded us of still more sober events that lie ahead: "As this work progresses in its onward course, and becomes more and more an object of political and religious interest and excitement, no king, ruler, or subject, no community or individual, will stand neutral. All will at length be influenced by one spirit or the other; and will take sides either for or against the kingdom of God."[9] On several occasions, President Ezra Taft Benson cited these words during general conference and indicated that we will see them fulfilled.[10]

President Joseph F. Smith has testified that the events of the Restoration have occurred in fulfillment of prophecy because the hand of the Lord is in this work. He said:

> The hand of the Lord may not be visible to all. There may be many who cannot discern the workings of God's will in the progress and development of this great latter-day work, but there are those who see in every hour and in every moment of the existence of the Church, from its beginning until now, the overruling, almighty hand of Him who sent His Only Begotten Son to the world to become a sacrifice for the sin of the world, that as He was lifted up so He, by reason of His righteousness and power and the sacrifice which He has made, might lift up unto God all the children of men who would hearken to His voice, receive His message, and obey His law.[11]

PROPHECIES YET TO BE FULFILLED

Besides all the past prophecies that have been fulfilled, there are other prophetic statements from modern prophets about the future prospects of the Lord's work. Consider the marvelous promises found in these statements.

John Taylor: "You will see the day that Zion will be as far ahead of the outside world in everything pertaining to learning of every kind as we are today in regard to religious matters. . . . God expects Zion to become the praise and glow of the whole earth, so that kings, hearing of her fame, will come and gaze upon her glory."[12]

John Taylor: "When Zion is established in her beauty and honor and glory, the kings and princes of the earth will come, in order that they may get information and teach the same to their people. They will come as they came to learn the wisdom of Solomon."[13]

Harold B. Lee similarly promised that if we would seek after and cultivate the fruits of the Spirit in our homes, the whole world would come knocking at our doors to have the same blessings: "I say to you Latter-day Saint mothers and fathers, if you will rise to the responsibility of teaching your children in the home—priesthood quorums preparing the fathers, the Relief Society the mothers—the day will soon be dawning when the whole world will come to our doors and will say, 'Show us your way that we may walk in your path.'"[14]

John Taylor: "We believe that there will be a temporal kingdom of God organized that will be under the direction and auspices of the Lord of Hosts, and that in all our affairs, whether they relate to things temporal or things spiritual, as we have been in the habit of calling them, we shall be under the direction of the Lord, as the Scriptures say, 'It shall come to pass that all the people shall be taught of the Lord.' This is part and parcel of our creed. We believe that we shall rear splendid edifices, magnificent temples and beautiful cities that shall become the pride, praise and glory of the whole earth. We believe that this people will excel in literature, in science and the arts and in manufactures. In fact, there will be a concentration of wisdom, not only of the combined wisdom of the world as it now exists, but men will be inspired in regard to all these matters in a manner and to an extent that they never have been before, and we shall have eventually, when the Lord's purposes are carried out, the most magnificent buildings, the most pleasant and beautiful gardens, the richest and most costly clothing, and be the most healthy and the most intellectual people that will reside upon the earth. This is part and parcel of our faith; in fact, Zion will become the praise of the whole earth; and as the Queen of Sheba said anciently, touching the glory of Solomon, the half of it had not been told her, so it will be in regard to Israel in their dwelling places. In fact, if there is anything great, noble, dignified, exalted, anything pure, or holy, or virtuous, or lovely, anything that is calculated to exalt or ennoble the human mind, to dignify and elevate the people, it will be found among the people of the Saints of the Most High God."[15]

Orson F. Whitney: "We will yet have Miltons and Shakespeares of our own. God's ammunition is not exhausted. His brightest spirits are held in reserve for the latter times. In God's name and by His help we will build up a literature whose top shall touch heaven. . . . Small things are the seeds of great things, and, like the acorn that brings forth the oak, or the snow-flake that forms the avalanche, God's kingdom will grow, and on wings of light and power soar to the summit of its destiny."[16]

The fulfillment of all these prophecies will be thrilling to witness. It is exciting to live in a day when prophecy, both ancient and modern, is being fulfilled.

Notes

1. Joseph Smith, *History of The Church of Jesus Christ of Latter-day Saints*, ed. B. H. Roberts, 2d ed. rev., 7 vols. (Salt Lake City: The Church of Jesus Christ of Latter-day Saints, 1980), 4:609

2. At the dedication of the LDS Conference Center, President Gordon B. Hinckley indicated that this marvelous hall fulfills Isaiah's prophecy: "As I contemplate this marvelous structure, adjacent to the temple, there comes to mind the great prophetic utterance of Isaiah: 'And it shall come to pass in the last days, that the mountain of the Lord's house shall be established in the top of

the mountains, and shall be exalted above the hills; and all nations shall flow unto it. And many people shall go and say, Come ye, and let us go up to the mountain of the Lord, to the house of the God of Jacob; and he will teach us of his ways, and we will walk in his paths: for out of Zion shall go forth the law, and the word of the Lord from Jerusalem. . . . O house of Jacob, come ye, and let us walk in the light of the Lord' (Isaiah 2:2–3, 5). I believe that prophecy applies to the historic and wonderful Salt Lake Temple. But I believe also that it is related to this magnificent hall. For it is from this pulpit that the law of God shall go forth, together with the word and testimony of the Lord" (Gordon B. Hinckley, "This Great Millennial Year," *Ensign,* November 2000, 69).

3. Joseph Smith, *Teachings of the Prophet Joseph Smith,* comp. Joseph Fielding Smith (Salt Lake City: Deseret Book, 1976), 366.

4. Heber J. Grant, in Conference Reports of The Church of Jesus Christ of Latter-day Saints (Salt Lake City: The Church of Jesus Christ of Latter-day Saints, 1898 to present), October 1919, 15.

5. Gordon B. Hinckley, "Look to the Future," *Ensign,* November 1997, 68.

6. George Q. Cannon, in *Journal of Discourses,* 26 vols. (London: Latter-day Saints' Book Depot, 1854–86), 19:105.

7. Orson Pratt, *Orson Pratt's Works* (Salt Lake City: Deseret News Press, 1945), 4.

8. George Q. Cannon, in *Journal of Discourses,* 19:105.

9. "Proclamation of the Twelve Apostles of The Church of Jesus Christ of Latter-day Saints," *Message of the First Presidency,* 1:257; see also Neal A. Maxwell, *Things As They Really Are* (Salt Lake City: Deseret Book, 1978), 60.

10. Ezra Taft Benson, "A Message to the World," *Ensign,* November 1975, 32–34; "May the Kingdom of God Go Forth," *Ensign,* May 1978, 32–34; "A Marvelous Work and a Wonder," *Ensign,* May 1980, 32–34.

11. Joseph F. Smith, in Conference Reports, April 1904, 2.

12. John Taylor, *The Gospel Kingdom* (Salt Lake City: Deseret Book, 1944), 275.

13. John Taylor, in *Journal of Discourses,* 6:169; see also *The Gospel Kingdom,* 216.

14. Harold B. Lee, in Conference Reports, October 1964, 87.

15. John Taylor, in *Journal of Discourses,* 10:146–67.

16. Orson F. Whitney, "Home Literature," *Contributor* 9, no. 8 (June 1888), 300.

CHAPTER NINE

FOURTH EVIDENCE FOR THE REALITY OF THE RESTORATION:

The Translation and Restoration of Scripture

A fourth evidence of the Restoration through Joseph Smith is his contribution to the canon of scripture. The Prophet Joseph, though unlearned and untrained in theology, has given the world more printed pages of scripture than any other individual. "As far as our records show, he has given us more revealed truth than any prophet who has ever lived upon the face of the earth,"[1] including more than Moses, Paul, Luke, and Mormon combined.[2] The revealing of new scripture, the restoration of ancient scripture, and the correction of mistranslated passages in the Bible places Joseph Smith in a unique station among biblical scholars.

In a revelation given the very day the Church was organized, the Lord declared that Joseph was a seer, *a translator*, a prophet, and an apostle of Jesus Christ (D&C 21:1). Unlike modern translators of ancient scriptures, the Prophet Joseph was called by direct revelation from the Savior to do the work of translation. It was a work the Lord "appointed" him to do (D&C 76:15).

THE ABILITY TO TRANSLATE—
A GIFT FROM GOD

The Book of Mormon prophet Alma noted that the Lord grants "unto all nations, of their own nation and tongue, to teach his word, yea, in wisdom, all that he seeth fit that they should have" (Alma 29:8). He grants that portion of His word to the children of men "according to the heed and diligence which they give unto him" (Alma 12:9). Thus, the ability to translate God's words into different languages is a gift from God, and Joseph Smith was blessed with that gift in an immense way.

It is a sobering responsibility to translate scripture. If an individual wishes to prove him-or herself a false prophet, all he or she need do is produce scripture and claim it is the revealed word of the Lord. For almost two centuries, Joseph Smith's revelations have been put to the test of their claim to authenticity and have never been found wanting.

St. Jerome (born Eusebius Hieronymous Sophronius, the first person to translate the Bible into Latin from the original Greek) once wrote of the difficult situation translators of God's words find themselves in:

> You urge me to make a new work out of an old one, and, as it were, to sit in judgement on the copies of the Scriptures now scattered throughout the whole world, and, since they differ from one another, to decide which of them agree with the true reading of the Greek original. The labour is one of love, but at the same time both perilous and presumptuous; for, in judging others, I must be myself judged by all. . . . Is there a man, learned or unlearned, who will not, when he takes the volume into his hands, and perceives that what he reads

does not suit his settled tastes, break out immediately into violent language, and call me a forger and a profane person for having the audacity to add anything to the ancient books, or to make any changes or corrections therein?[3]

To illustrate the principle of translation as a gift from God, consider the experience of Priscilla Sampson-Davis who received a copy of the Book of Mormon in Ghana in 1963. She studied it and was converted to the Church and shortly after her baptism had a vision that she described in these words:

I wasn't asleep. I saw myself at a sacrament meeting and we were singing when I saw a personage in very bright apparel standing in front of the congregation. The Personage called me by name and requested that I come and stand by Him. . . . He then asked me why some were not singing with the others. I told him that they could not read English. . . . He asked me if I wouldn't like to help my sisters and brothers sing praises to our Heavenly Father. I said that I would do my best. Then the vision passed away. Immediately I . . . started translating the hymn *Redeemer of Israel* into Fanti [the major dialect in Ghana].

Sister Sampson-Davis translated the hymns, the missionary pamphlets, and Gospel Principles. Then, under assignment, she translated the Book of Mormon, the Doctrine and Covenants, and the Pearl of Great Price into Fanti. She said, "It was the Lord Himself who commissioned me to do the translation. . . . By translating these things, my brothers and sisters who can't understand English will be able to see and read the true gospel for themselves."[4]

The Book of Mormon teaches that "a seer is a revelator and a prophet also; and. . . . a seer can know of things which are past, and also of things which are to come, and by [him] shall all things be revealed, or, rather, shall secret things be made manifest, and hidden things shall come to light, and things which are not known shall be made known by [him] which otherwise could not be known. . . . therefore he becometh a great benefit to his fellow beings" (Mosiah 8:16–18). Truly, Joseph Smith was one of the great seers, prophets, and translators to live on this earth, whose written revelations have proven to be "a great benefit to his fellow beings."

EXAMPLES OF THE ANCIENT RECORDS JOSEPH SMITH TRANSLATED OR RESTORED

There are too many examples of Joseph's abilities as a seer while working with scripture that could be cited. Some of the scriptures Joseph gave the world were translated from ancient texts by the gift and power of God. Others were revealed in visions. All are profound.

In just fifteen years (from 1829, when the Book of Mormon was translated, until 1844, when Joseph Smith was martyred), the Prophet Joseph gave the world more printed pages of scripture than found anywhere in the world, including the following.

The Book of Mormon. At 531 pages, this is the largest book of scripture ever revealed at one time. Using the Urim and Thummim, Joseph Smith translated the Book of Mormon in sixty to seventy-five days when he was only twenty-three years old. His wife, Emma Smith, stated that at the time "Joseph Smith could neither write nor dictate a coherent and well-worded letter; let alone dictating a book like the Book of Mormon."[5] The Prophet Joseph said it is "the most correct of any book on earth, and the keystone of our religion, and a man would get nearer to God by abiding by its precepts than by any other book."[6] Like the Old and New Testaments, the Book of Mormon is "Another Testament" that Jesus is the Christ and one of the greatest testaments ever produced proclaiming His divinity.[7]

Writings of John the Beloved. Another record Joseph translated was a parchment written by John the Revelator and hidden by him. Using the Urim and Thummim, Joseph was allowed to see the parchment and translate it without having the writing in front of him (D&C 7).

In 1833, Joseph received by revelation a testimony John the Beloved recorded of what he had heard John the Baptist teach (D&C 93:6-18). In it John promised that one day the full record of John the Baptist's testimony will be revealed (D&C 93:6, 18).

Writings and histories of Moses, Adam, Enoch, and Noah. From June 1830 to February 1831, Joseph Smith received several visions while using the Urim and Thummim. These were compiled into the book of Moses and contains: several visions of Moses (Moses 1–5); a revelation of the Gospel to Adam (Moses 6); a prophecy of Enoch (Moses 6–7); and a history of Noah (Moses 8).

The Book of Abraham. Another scriptural record restored by the Prophet Joseph was a record about Father Abraham now found in the Pearl of Great Price. Joseph Smith's book of Abraham contains unique stories about the patriarch Abraham that do not appear in any Bible texts. Abraham is the Father of the Faithful to three great world religions: Christianity, Judaism, and Islam. If a person wanted to prove himself a fraud in the religious world, all he'd have to do is make up stories about Abraham. Interestingly, though, all of the stories Joseph Smith included in his book about Abraham have since been discovered numerous times in various non-biblical sources.[8] Beyond coincidence, this is an absolute evidence of divine design in the book of Abraham Joseph Smith was inspired to reveal.

The Joseph Smith Translation (JST) of the Bible. Joseph Smith also gave us an inspired translation of the King James version of the Bible. His translation contains hundreds of corrections to mistranslated verses and numerous additions to the text. His work with the Bible fulfills prophecy (Moses 1:40–41). The JST corrects false doctrines that have arisen from faulty interpretations. Joseph said, "I will now turn linguist. There are many things in the Bible which do not, as they now stand, accord with the revelations of the Holy Ghost to me."[9] Joseph made this assessment of the text of the Bible: "I believe the Bible as it read when it came from the pen of the original writers. Ignorant translators, careless transcribers, or designing and corrupt priests have commit-ted many errors."[10] In the Joseph Smith Translation of the Bible, many "plain and precious" things have been restored. The Savior indicated that the changes made in the JST of the Bible are recorded "even as they are in mine own bosom, to the salvation of mine own elect" (D&C 35:20). The JST was first published in 1867 by the RLDS Church, and then in 1979, the most doctrinally significant portions of the JST were published in the LDS edition of the scriptures.

New Revelations. In addition to all other scriptures, Joseph also wrote a personal history of the Church and included many revelations he had received about the Resto-ration. Many of these were canonized in the Doctrine and Covenants as scripture. Joseph never expected the people to believe in his revelations without putting them to the test. On one occasion, he said, "Search the scriptures—search the revelations which we publish, and ask your Heavenly

Father, in the name of His Son Jesus Christ, to manifest the truth unto you, and if you do it with an eye single to His glory nothing doubting, He will answer you by the power of His Holy Spirit. You will then know for yourselves and not for another. You will not then be dependent on man for the knowledge of God; nor will there be any room for speculation. No; for when men receive their instruction from Him that made them, they know how He will save them. Then again we say: Search the Scriptures, search the Prophets and learn what portion of them belongs to you and the people of the nineteenth century."[11]

Regarding one of the greatest revelations ever recorded—a revelation to Joseph Smith about the afterlife and the various degrees of glory we can inherit in the resurrection (D&C 76)—Joseph noted:

> Nothing could be more pleasing to the Saints upon the order of the Kingdom of the Lord, than the light which burst upon the world through the foregoing vision. Every law, every commandment, every promise, every truth, and every point touching the destiny of man, from Genesis to Revelation, where the purity of the scriptures remains unsullied by the folly of men, go to show the perfection of the theory [of different degrees of glory in the future life] and witnesses the fact *that the document is a transcript from the records of the eternal world.* The sublimity of the ideas; the purity of the language; the scope for action; the continued duration for completion, in order that the heirs of salvation may confess the Lord and bow the knee; the rewards for faithfulness, and the punishments for sins, are so much beyond the narrow-mindedness of

men, that every honest man is constrained to exclaim: "It came from God."[12]

Any one of the above-mentioned texts or modern revelations would prove a man to be a divinely inspired restorer of truth. What, then, are we to say about a man who brought them all forward within a period of fifteen years? The translation, restoration, and publication of scripture is one of the great evidences that the Restoration came through the Prophet Joseph Smith.

Wilford Woodruff described the feelings of the Saints at receiving so much additional scripture: "Truly the Lord has raised up Joseph the Seer . . . & is now clothing him with mighty power & wisdom and knowledge. . . . The Lord is Blessing Joseph with Power to reveal the mysteries of the kingdom of God; to translate through the Urim & Thummim Ancient records & Hyeroglyphics [sic] as old as Abraham or Adam, which causes our hearts to burn within us while we behold their glorious truths opened unto us."[13]

Elder Bruce R. McConkie summarized the Latter-day Saint view of the Bible and Joseph Smith's authority to bring forth new scriptures:

> There are no people on earth who hold the Bible in such high esteem as we do. We believe it, we read and ponder its sayings, we rejoice in the truths it teaches, and we seek to conform our lives to the divine standard it proclaims. But we do not believe, as does evangelical Christianity, that the Bible contains all things necessary for salvation; nor do we believe that God has now taken upon himself the tongue of the dumb which no longer speaks, nor reveals, nor makes known his will to his children. Indeed, we know that

the Bible contains only a sliver, a twig, a leaf, no more than a small branch at most, from the great redwood of revelation that God has given in ages past. There has been given ten thousand times ten thousand more revelation than has been preserved for us in our present Bible. It contains a bucket, a small pail, a few draughts, no more than a small stream at most, out of the great ocean of revealed truth that has come to men in ages more spiritually enlightened than ours.[14]

The prodigious amount of scripture restored by the Prophet Joseph Smith is illustrated in the following chart:

Document	Date Written	Date Restored	Method of Translation
1. The Book of Mormon	2200 B.C.– 421 A.D.	22 Sept. 1827	Translation— Urim and Thummim
2. Parchment of John (D&C 7)	96–100 A.D.	April 1829	Translation— Urim and Thummim (without having parchment)
3. Visions of Moses (Moses 1)	1300 B.C.	June 1830	Revelation to Joseph Smith
4. Revelation to Enoch of the Gospel of Adam (Moses 6:43–63)	4000 B.C.	Dec. 1830	Revelation to Joseph Smith

Document	Date Written	Date Restored	Method of Translation
5. Prophecy of Enoch (Moses 6:1–42; 7:1–69)	3003 B.C.	Dec. 1830	Revelation to Joseph Smith
6. Revelation to Moses about the Creation (Moses 2:1–5:59)	1250 B.C.	Dec. 1830	Revelation to Joseph Smith
7. History of Noah (Moses 8:1–30)	2350 B.C.	Dec. 1830	Revelation to Joseph Smith
8. Joseph Smith–Matthew (JST of Matthew 24)	33–90 A.D.	March 1830–Feb. 1833	Joseph Smith Translation (June 1830–2 July 1833; published in 1867 by the RLDS Church)
9. Record of Abraham	2000–1859 B.C.	July 1835	Translation inspired by Egyptian papyrus
10. Record of Joseph	1700 B.C.	July 1835	Interpretation of some characters by Joseph Smith. Complete record never provided.
11. Record of John the Baptist written by John the Revelator (D&C 93:6–18)	Approximately 90 A.D.	6 May 1833	Revelation to Joseph Smith

Notes

1. Elder LeGrand P. Richards, in Conference Reports of The Church of Jesus Christ of Latter-day Saints (Salt Lake City: The Church of Jesus Christ of Latter-day Saints, 1898 to present), April 1981, 43.

2. Elder Neal A. Maxwell, "A Choice Seer," *Speeches*, ed. Karen Seely (Provo, Utah: University Publications, 1986), 113.

3. *Creeds, Councils and Controversies, Documents Illustrating the History of the Church A.D. 337–461*, ed. J. Stevenson (Cambridge: University Press, 1989), 183.

4. E. Dale LeBaron, "African Converts without Baptism: A Unique and Inspiring Chapter in Church History," BYU Devotional, 3 November 1998, 13.

5. "Last Testimony of Sister Emma," *Saints' Herald* (October 1879): 289–90; as cited in Royal Skousen, "Towards a Critical Edition of the Book of Mormon," *BYU Studies* (Winter 1990): 51.

6. Joseph Smith, *History of The Church of Jesus Christ of Latter-day Saints,* ed. B. H. Roberts, 2d ed. rev., 7 vols. (Salt Lake City: The Church of Jesus Christ of Latter-day Saints, 1980), 4:461.

7. The Book of Mormon mentions the Savior more times per verse than even the New Testament (Susan Ward Easton, "Discovery," *Ensign,* July 1978, 60).

8. *Traditions about the Early Life of Abraham,* comp. and ed. John A. Tvedtnes, Brian M. Hauglid, and John Gee (Provo, Utah: FARMS, 2001).

9. Joseph Smith, *Teachings of the Prophet Joseph Smith,* comp. Joseph Fielding Smith (Salt Lake City: Deseret Book, 1976), 310.

10. Ibid., 327.

11. Ibid., 11–12.

12. Smith, *History of the Church,* 1:252–53; emphasis added.

13. Willford Woodruff, *Wilford Woodruff's Journals,* ed. Scott G. Kenney (Midvale, Utah: Signature Books, 1983), 19 February 1842.

14. Bruce R. McConkie, "The Bible: A Sealed Book," Eighth Annual Church Education System Religious Educators' Symposium–New Testament Supplement (Salt Lake City: The Church of Jesus Christ of Latter-day Saints, 1984), 31.

CHAPTER TEN

FIFTH EVIDENCE FOR THE REALITY OF THE RESTORATION:

The Restoration of True Doctrine and the Plan of Salvation

A fifth evidence of the Prophet's role in the Restoration is the restoration of true doctrine. Because there is no salvation in false doctrine, mankind has asked what needs to be done to lay hold on eternal life. Joseph understood that the same doctrines and ordinances instituted in the heavens before the foundation of the world for the salvation of men and women would always be the same for everyone.

As Elder George Q. Cannon noted, there is only one straight and narrow path leading to God: "There are no two modes of baptism, there are no two methods of organizing the Church of Christ; there are no two paths leading into the kingdom of God our heavenly Father; there are no two forms of doctrine. 'There is one Lord,' as the Apostle Paul says, 'one faith and one baptism.'"[1] Elder Cannon continued this line of reasoning by teaching that the same revealed principles that saved ancient peoples will save us. It should not be surprising, therefore, that if Joseph Smith was teaching the truth, it would harmonize perfectly with the ancient order of things:

> There is one form of doctrine, and when
> we all meet, (those of us who shall be so
> fortunate as to be redeemed and sanctified in

the presence of our Father and the Lamb,) we shall find that our doctrines will precisely agree; our obedience will be of a similar character, we shall all discover that the doctrines that we have received and bowed in submission to are precisely the same doctrines, whether we were baptized into Christ in America, in Asia, in Africa or any other part of the earth, and it will be found when we all come together, (that is the family of our heavenly Father,) that we have all received the same faith, the same doctrines, and have partaken of the same Spirit and the same gifts, the Spirit having rested down upon all alike according to his or her faith. If it were not so heaven would be full of clashing sectaries; it would be full of confusion, strife and division and every kind of contention; because the same spirit that characterizes men here, and that creates division and contention among them here, if they could reach heaven in the possession of it, as some claim they do, would turn heaven itself into a pandemonium, and make it no better than this earth so far as confusion is concerned. This is not the Gospel of the Lord Jesus; this is not the path that he marked out. He marked out a plain path and all the inhabitants of the earth must, if they ever come into the presence of the Lamb, walk in that path to the end, or they never can reach there.[2]

Joseph Smith restored the knowledge that our Father in Heaven has a plan for our eternal salvation. He revealed that we were taught this plan in the premortal life and that this great plan includes the eternal principles, doctrines, and ordinances necessary for exaltation. It is centered in the atonement and resurrection of Jesus Christ—without which, redemption and salvation would not be possible (Mosiah 3:17). Even though there exists a "great plan of happiness" for our redemption (Alma 42:8, 16), the word *plan* does not appear in the Old or New Testaments. One could read the entire Bible, cover to cover, and possibly not know there was a plan, let alone the details.[3] Although the doctrines and ordinances of the plan are taught, or alluded to, in the Bible, no one in all of Christian history has ever clarified the plan of salvation as plainly as it was revealed to Joseph Smith. He called it "one of heaven's best gifts to mankind."[4] He correctly observed that it is only reasonable that God would reveal something to us about the meaning and purpose of life:

> All men know that they must die. And it is important that we understand the reasons and causes of our exposure to the vicissitudes of life and of death, and the designs and purposes of God in our coming into the world, our sufferings here, and our departure hence. What is the object of our coming into existence, then dying and falling away, to be here no more? It is but reasonable to suppose that God would reveal something in reference to the matter, and it is a subject we ought to study more than any other. We ought to study it day and night, for the world is ignorant in reference to their true condition and relation. If we have any claim on our Heavenly Father for anything, it is for knowledge on this important subject.[5]

Here are some of the phrases revealed by the Lord to Joseph Smith about His plan for our salvation. Note the variety of ways the Lord describes His marvelous plan:

• The plan of redemption (Alma 12:26, 30, 32–33; 17:16; 18:39; 29:2; 39:18; 42:11, 13).

• The great plan of redemption (Jacob 6:8; Alma 34:31).

• The great and eternal plan of redemption (Alma 34:16).

• The plan of redemption prepared from the foundation of the world (Alma 12:25; 22:13).

• The plan of salvation (Jarom 1:2; Alma 24:14; Moses 6:62).

• The great plan of salvation (Alma 42:5).

• The plan of happiness (Alma 42:16).

• The great plan of happiness (Alma 42:8).

• The plan of mercy (Alma 42:15).

• The great plan of mercy (Alma 42:31).

• The plan of restoration (Alma 41:2).

• The great and eternal plan of deliverance (2 Nephi 11:5).

• God's eternal plan (D&C Official Declaration 2).

• The great plan of the eternal God (Alma 34:9).

• The merciful plan of the Great Creator (2 Nephi 9:6).

• How great the plan of our God (2 Nephi 9:13).

Some examples of the doctrines belonging to the plan of salvation that are spoken of in the Bible but that were restored and amplified by Joseph Smith include the following. Not all the verses related to each topic were included in this chart. The verses listed merely serve to illustrate how in tune Joseph Smith's revelations were with the doctrinal teachings of ancient prophets:

Bible Reference	Doctrine	Latter-day Revelations
Jeremiah 1:5	The premortal existence	D&C 93:29; Abr. 3:22–23
Luke 23:43	The post-earthly spirit paradise	Alma 40:11–12
1 Peter 3:19; 4:6	The post-earthly spirit prison	Alma 40:13–14
1 Corinthians 15:40 (JST)	The three degrees of glory in the resurrection	D&C 76:70–109; 131:1–4
1 Corinthians 15:29	Baptism for the dead (providing ordinances for those who lived on earth at times or in places where the gospel was not to be found so that all may receive an opportunity for salvation)	D&C 128:16–18
Amos 3:7	Revelation to living prophets	1 Nephi 22:1–2; D&C 1:17; 21:1, 5

Bible Reference	Doctrine	Latter-day Revelations
Acts 8:17	Receiving the Holy Ghost by the laying on of hands by those with priesthood authority	D&C 20:41, 43; 35:6; 39:23
Matthew 3:16–17	The doctrine of the Godhead (the Father, Son, and Holy Ghost are three separate personages)	D&C 130:22; JS–H 1:17, 25
Luke 24:39	Christ had a body of flesh and bones after the Resurrection	D&C 130:22
1 Corinthians 15:20–22	The literal resurrection of all mankind	D&C 88:14–31
Genesis 1:26–27	Men and women are created in God's image	Ether 3:15; D&C 20:18; Moses 6:8–9
Matthew 16:19	Sealing power of the priesthood (enables ordinances performed in mortality to be valid in heaven)	D&C 110:13–16; 132:7
Romans 8:17	We are literal children of God and can become like our Heavenly Father	D&C 88:107; 93:20; 132:20–24

As one looks at this sampling of restored doctrines, it is interesting to remember Joseph Smith's response when asked, "Wherein do you differ from other sects?" He answered, "In that we believe the Bible."[6] Joseph later testified: "In this sacred volume [the Bible] . . . the 'Mormon' faith is to be found. We teach nothing but what the Bible teaches. We believe nothing, but what is to be found in this book."[7]

But Joseph was not limited to what was recorded in the Bible. He had revealed to him more information that helps elucidate these doctrines. By comparing what was revealed to Joseph Smith to any topic found in the Bible, greater understanding and clarity will result. This exercise holds true for any principle of the Gospel of Jesus Christ. What he received is both mind-expanding and soul-satisfying.

FOREVER FAMILIES

One of the greatest doctrines restored through the Prophet Joseph regards the eternal nature of family relations—that family relationships endure beyond the grave: "When the Savior shall appear . . . that same sociality which exists among us here will exist among us there, only it will be coupled with eternal glory, which glory we do not now enjoy" (D&C 130:1–2). The love we feel for one another endures, not by virtue of the love that binds us heart to heart, but because priesthood authority and sealing keys were restored to the Prophet Joseph that can make valid in heaven the marriages performed by priesthood authority on earth (Matthew 16:19; D&C 132:19–24). The restored gospel of Jesus Christ teaches us that there are no temporary relationships. It reminds us that we are eternal beings, literal children of God.

Elder Parley P. Pratt described his joy when he first learned this doctrine from the Prophet Joseph. He said that the Prophet had "lifted a corner of the veil and given me a single glance into eternity":

> It was Joseph Smith who taught me how to prize the endearing relationships of father and mother, husband and wife; of brother and sister, son and daughter.
>
> It was from him that I learned that the wife of my bosom might be secured to me for time and all eternity; and that the refined

sympathies and affections which endeared us to each other emanated from the fountain of divine eternal love. It was from him that I learned that we might cultivate these affections, and grow and increase in the same to all eternity. . . .

I had loved before, but I knew not why. But now I loved—with a pureness—an intensity of elevated, exalted feeling, which would lift my soul from the transitory things of this grovelling sphere and expand it as the ocean. I felt that God was my heavenly Father indeed; that Jesus was my brother, and that the wife of my bosom was an immortal, eternal companion; . . . In short, I could now love with the spirit and with the understanding also.[8]

The doctrines Joseph Smith restored are complete and truly edifying. We do believe in the Bible. We understand and love the doctrines taught in the Bible. We do not ask anyone to give up their belief or faith in this great book but to come and receive more. Those who love the Bible will love the doctrines of the Restoration as revealed through the Prophet Joseph Smith.

Notes

1. George Q. Cannon, in *Journal of Discourses*, 26 vols. (London: Latter-day Saints' Book Depot, 1854–86), 19:105.

2. Ibid., 19:105–6.

3. Regarding this point, President Harold B. Lee once said, "A short while ago I came across an interesting statement from Napoleon the First . . . : 'I would believe in a religion if it existed even since the beginning of time, but when I consider Socrates later than Mohammed I no longer believe. All religions have been made by men.' Think about that. When did the church and kingdom of

God on earth begin? Did it begin on April 6, 1830? If so, what about the millions who lived in the thousands of years prior to the restoration of the Gospel? Were not they entitled to this power to gain the mastery over self to live eternally? And so Napoleon would be right. . . . How old is the gospel upon the earth? Did it commence now in our days, or did it have a beginning prior to our days? This is what the Prophet Joseph Smith said about that: 'Some say that the kingdom of God was not set upon the earth until the Day of Pentecost [that was following the death of the Master], and that John did not preach the Baptism of Repentance for the remission of sins, but I say, in the name of the Lord, that the Kingdom was set up on the earth from the day of Adam to the present time. Whenever there has been a righteous man upon the earth to whom God revealed His word and gave power and authority to administer in His name, and where there is a priest of God, a minister who has power and authority from God to administer in the ordinances of the Gospel and officiate in the Priesthood of God, there is the kingdom of God.' (*Teachings*, 271). . . . The 'Gospel' is as old as the first man upon this earth. It has been here in dispensations. There has been the power to teach men the way to live, ever since the beginning of man upon this earth, else what Napoleon says would be true in this case as it is of every other church which has no claim upon such antiquity" (Harold B. Lee, "The Glory of God Is Intelligence," CES Summer School at Brigham Young University, 1954; typescript in possession of author).

4. Joseph Smith, *Teachings of the Prophet Joseph Smith*, comp. Joseph Fielding Smith (Salt Lake City: Deseret Book, 1976), 68.

5. Ibid., 324.

6. Ibid., 119.

7. Joseph Smith, *History of The Church of Jesus Christ of Latter-day Saints*, ed. B. H. Roberts, 2d ed. rev., 7 vols. (Salt Lake City: The Church of Jesus Christ of Latter-day Saints, 1980), 4:78.

8. Parley P. Pratt, *The Autobiography of Parley P. Pratt*, ed. Parley P. Pratt Jr. (Salt Lake City: Deseret Book, 1985), 259–60.

CHAPTER ELEVEN

SIXTH EVIDENCE FOR THE
REALITY OF THE RESTORATION:

The Restoration of the Savior's Church

A sixth evidence of the Restoration through the Prophet Joseph is the organization of The Church of Jesus Christ of Latter-day Saints. There are numerous examples of offices and orders of the priesthood described in the Bible, which are today found in the Church restored by Joseph Smith. These priesthood offices and authority delineated in the Old and New Testaments have long been lost to mankind. Joseph Smith not only restored these very offices but also gave detailed descriptions of the duties, rights, and blessings associated with them, as illustrated in the following chart:

Bible Reference	Priesthood Office/ Authority	Modern Revelation
Hebrews 7:11	Aaronic Priesthood	D&C 13; 84:18, 26–27, 30; 107:13–14, 20
Hebrews 6:20	Melchizedek Priesthood	D&C 84:19– 22, 33–42; 107:1–8, 18–19
1 Timothy 3:8–13	Deacons	D&C 20:38, 57–59; 107:85
1 Cor. 12:28; Ephesians 4:11	Teachers	D&C 20:53– 60; 107:86
Exodus 19:6	Priests	D&C 20:46–52

Bible Reference	Priesthood Office/ Authority	Modern Revelation
Exodus 24:9	Elders	D&C 20:38–45
James 5:14–15	Elders using oil to bless the sick	D&C 42:43–44; 66:9
1 Timothy 3:1–7	Bishops	D&C 20:67; 107:17
Hebrews 5:10	High priests	D&C 107:10, 12, 17
Ephesians 4:11	Patriarchs	D&C 107:39; 124:91–92; Evangelist, Bible Dictionary
Luke 10:1	Seventies	D&C 107:25–26, 34, 93–98
Ephesians 2:20; 4:11–14	Apostles and prophets	D&C 107:22–24, 33, 35, 39, 58; 112:30–32

As Elder Bruce R. McConkie has explained, "Our Lord's true Church is the formal, official organization of believers who have taken upon themselves the name of Christ by baptism, thus covenanting to serve God and keep his commandments. (D. & C. 10:67–69; 18:20–25.) It is literally the kingdom of God on earth (D. & C. 65; 84:34; 136:41), and as such its affairs are administered by apostles, prophets, and other legal administrators appointed by Christ the King. (1 Cor. 12:27–29.). . . . *Those who join the true Church and keep their covenants gain salvation in the celestial kingdom of God.* (D. & C. 10:55, 69.) In the true Church there will be apostles, prophets, true doctrinal teachings, revelation, visions, miracles, healings, the ministering of angels, and all of the gifts of the Spirit. (Mark 16:14–20; 1 Cor. 12; 13;

14; 3 Ne. 27; Morm. 8; 9; Moro. 7; 8; D. & C. 46.) Where these things are found, there is the true Church; where these things are not found, there the true Church is not."[1]

The reestablishment of God's true Church on the earth in these latter days was an important event of eternal significance. The Church was organized according to the pattern revealed by the Lord "for the perfecting of the Saints . . . till we all come in the unity of the faith, and of the knowledge of the Son of God" (Ephesians 4:12–13). Any person can organize a church, but as Elder LeGrand Richards observed, "How can they put in it the power and the authority to act in the name of the Lord?"[2] The restoration of the Church could not be accomplished by committees or creeds or by simple realignment of existing religions. It required revelation from on high.

THE CHURCH AND KINGDOM OF GOD ALWAYS REVEALED FROM HEAVEN

The gospel and Church of Jesus Christ was first organized in the days of Adam and Eve, with the great patriarch, Adam, standing at its head.[3] The divine pattern for organizing the Church was established from the beginning—the true church has always been revealed by the Lord: "And thus the Gospel began to be preached, from the beginning, being declared by holy angels sent forth from the presence of God, and by his own voice, and by the gift of the Holy Ghost" (Moses 5:58). Joseph Smith similarly testified that "we never can comprehend the things of God and heaven, but by revelation."[4] As the Prophet Jacob declared, "Great and marvelous are the works of the Lord. How unsearchable are the depths of the mysteries of him . . . and *no man knoweth of his ways save it be revealed unto him; wherefore . . .* despise not the revelations of God" (Jacob 4:8).

Accordingly, the first principles and ordinances of the Gospel of Jesus Christ were revealed to Adam and Eve, who taught their children about the absolute necessity of faith in the Lord Jesus Christ, repentance, baptism by immersion, and receiving the gift of the Holy Ghost by the laying on of hands (Moses 6:51–58).

THE FINAL RESTORATION

Through the centuries, many have recognized that elements once present in the original church were missing. For hundreds of years, reformers sought to bring back what was once present—including the offices and authority of the priesthood, the organization of the Church of Jesus Christ, and the gifts of the Spirit that were exercised anciently as described in the Bible. No individual nor council was able to recover what was lost until the Father and the Son appeared to Joseph Smith to inaugurate the "restitution of all things, which God hath spoken by the mouth of all his holy prophets since the world began" (Acts 3:21).

From heavenly beings, the gospel was restored to the Prophet Joseph Smith, and the promise was given by the Lord that it would never be taken from the earth again nor given to another people (D&C 27:13). The ministering of angels continued, and Joseph Smith and Oliver Cowdery received the Aaronic Priesthood by the laying on of hands from John the Baptist (D&C 13) and the Melchizedek Priesthood in the same manner from Peter, James, and John (D&C 128:20)

Later, while translating the Book of Mormon, Joseph Smith received a commandment from the Lord to "organize His Church once more here upon the earth." Joseph was told not only the "precise day upon which, according to His will and commandment, we should proceed"[5] (April 6, 1830) but was also informed by revelation how to conduct the organizational meeting.[6] The restoration of the true Church of Jesus Christ was sanctioned by God; it was restored under the Savior's direction through a living prophet in harmony with the prophet Amos's inspired declaration: "Surely the Lord will do nothing until he revealeth his secret unto his servants the prophets" (JST Amos 3:7).

APRIL 6—A UNIQUE AND WONDERFUL DAY

April 6 may well be the most significant date in world history. As President Charles W. Nibley exclaimed, "A wonderful day, the sixth day of April! Many notable things have occurred on it."[7] This is the day the Savior was born in Bethlehem,[8] when heavenly hosts declared the glad tidings: "For unto you is born this day in the city of David a Saviour, who is Christ the Lord" (JST Luke 2:11). The Prophet Joseph Smith indicated that he believed the Savior's death and resurrection also occurred around April 6.[9]

Because the Savior's "true and living" Church (D&C 1:30) was organized on April 6, this further sets that day apart as the day the foundation for the salvation of all mankind was established—an event of such vital significance that every person who now lives, who has ever lived, and who will yet live will be effected by it. As President Ezra Taft Benson has observed, "The greatest events of history are those which affect the greatest number for the longest periods."[10] That being true, then April 6 qualifies as the greatest date in human history.

According to the Savior's revealed instructions, and under the Prophet Joseph Smith's direction, a small group gathered in the log house of Peter and Mary Whitmer in Fayette, New York, to organize the Lord's Church. This humble one-and-a-half story log house, measuring twenty feet by thirty feet, with hand-made shingles and hand-made nails has to be the most unique home in all the world. This is where the translation of the Book of Mormon was completed (Joseph, Emma, and Oliver Cowdery had lived with the Whitmers in 1829 while they completed the translation of the Book of Mormon); the Three Witnesses (Oliver Cowdery, David Whitmer, and Martin Harris with Joseph Smith) saw the angel Moroni, who showed them the Book of Mormon plates; the Church of Jesus Christ was organized; and where more than half of the revelations—now canonized in the Doctrine and Covenants—were received by Joseph Smith.

On April 6, 1830, the Church was originally named *The Church of Jesus Christ*, and in an 1838 revelation the name was designated as *The Church of Jesus Christ of Latter-day Saints* (D&C 115:1–4).

GROWTH IN CHURCH ORGANIZATION

Following the April 6 meeting, the Lord revealed the full organization of His Church line upon line. He commanded Joseph Smith to begin a systematic and intense study of the Bible.[11] The effort occupied much of his time for the next three years.

While studying the Bible, the Lord revealed to the Prophet Joseph expansive understanding about the offices and organization of the Church. Dr. Robert J. Matthews has noted the significant role the Joseph Smith Translation of the Bible played in establishing the Church of Jesus Christ following the first organizational meeting. The restoration of doctrines, ordinances, and priesthood offices was not incidental to the Joseph Smith's work translating the Bible—it was in consequence of it.

Consider what the Church was like in 1830. What were the offices, the doctrines, and the practices of the Church in that day? It would be easier to describe what was not yet a part of the Church. In June 1830 there no wards, no stakes, no First Presidency, no Council of the Twelve, no patriarchs, no seventies, no bishops, no "Word of Wisdom," no revelation on the degrees of glory, no tithing, no welfare program, no law of consecration [or united order], no priesthood quorums of any kind, no temples, no endowments, no sealings, no marriages for eternity, no real understanding of the New Jerusalem, no baptisms for the dead, no Doctrine and Covenants, no Pearl of Great Price, and no Joseph Smith Translation [of the Bible]. How did these things, which today we recognize as vital to our spiritual life and as basic to the Church, come to be? They came when the time was right and in answer to prayer—the result of earnest search. Each of these things was revealed at some time and place and in some particular situation; and each became, one-by-one, part of the doctrine and structure of the Church. Many of the fundamental doctrines of the gospel which are contained in the Doctrine and Covenants were first made known to the Prophet Joseph Smith as he worked through the pages of the Bible while making his inspired translation.[12]

In an 1846 letter to a friend, Oliver Cowdery described the anticipatory feelings of excitement and hope that filled the hearts of those who attended the 1830 organizational meeting of the Church. He wrote, "You say you are having a meeting on the 6th of April. Brother Phineas, I could be with you, and tell you about the 6th of April 1830, when but six men then only belonged to the Church, and how we looked forward to the future."[13]

Sidney Rigdon recalled the same spirit and feeling that attended them all immediately following the organization of the Church: "I met the whole church of Christ in a little old log house about 20 feet square, near Waterloo, N.Y. and we began to talk about the kingdom of God as if we had the world at our command; we talked with great confidence, and talked big things, although we were not many people, we had big feelings; . . . we were as big then, as we shall ever be; we began to talk like men in authority and power; . . . we saw by vision, the church of God, a thousand times larger. . . . Many things were taught, believed, and preached, then, which have since come to pass; . . . if we had talked in public, we should have been ridiculed more than we were, the world being entirely ignorant of the testimony of the prophets and without knowledge of what God was about to do."[14]

THE RESTORATION IS REASONABLE AND SCRIPTURAL

Because of the divine revelation given through the Prophet Joseph, Latter-day Saints profess to have all the officers, gifts, and authority to administer in every ordinance and blessing of the ancient Church. Joseph Smith's doctrine is reasonable; it is scriptural and infallible in its precepts, ordinances, and gifts, as Elder Orson Pratt insightfully noted:

If Joseph Smith were an impostor, whence his superior wisdom? What power inspired his mind in laying the foundation of a church according to the ancient order? How could an impostor so far surpass the combined wisdom of seventeen centuries as to originate a system diverse from every other system under heaven, and yet harmonize with the system of Jesus and His apostles in every particular? . . . against which not one scriptural argument can be adduced! The idea is preposterous! The purity and infallibility of the doctrine of this great modern prophet is a presumptive evidence of no small moment in favor of his divine mission. . . . For a young man, inexperienced and illiterate, to profess to give the word of the Lord upon subjects of so great a moment—to reveal doctrines which were directly opposed, not only to his own traditions, but to the teachings and doctrines of the most popular, numerous, and powerful sects of the day, and at the same time have those doctrines exactly accord, not only with the ancient gospel, but with every minute prediction relative to the dispensation of the last days, is an evidence that carries truth upon the face of it, and leaves a deep and lasting impression upon every reflecting mind, and we can hardly refrain from assenting in our hearts, that surely he must have been sent of God.[15]

The restoration by revelation and the organization of the Lord's Church on April 6, 1830, and its subsequent development, was accomplished in harmony with five eternal principles. It was done (1) in agreement with the laws of the land, (2) by the consent of the people, (3) with the authority of the holy priesthood, (4) according to the will of God, and (5) by divine revelation and directive. It will therefore roll on, as Daniel prophesied, until it fills the whole earth (Daniel

2:34–35). It will be preached to all nations, as the Savior declared: "This gospel of the kingdom shall be preached in all the world for a witness unto all nations; and then shall the end come" (Matthew 24:14). And though it may be few in number, compared to other organizations, it will eventually cover the entire earth just as the ancient prophets Enoch and Nephi foresaw (Moses 7:62; 1 Nephi 14:12).

The restored Church of Jesus Christ now makes salvation and exaltation attainable for all who desire eternal life.

Notes

1. Bruce R. McConkie, *Mormon Doctrine,* 2d ed. (Salt Lake City: Bookcraft, 1966), 133–34.

2. LeGrand Richards, "The True Church," *Ensign,* July 1972, 114.

3. Mark E. Petersen, *Adam: Who Is He?* (Salt Lake City: Deseret Book, 1976), 66; Bruce R. McConkie, *Mormon Doctrine,* 133; "Prophets," *Encyclopedia of Mormonism,* 4 vols., ed. Daniel H. Ludlow (New York: Macmillan, 1992), 3:1165.

4. Joseph Smith, *Teachings of the Prophet Joseph Smith,* comp. Joseph Fielding Smith (Salt Lake City: Deseret Book, 1976), 292.

5. Joseph Smith, *History of The Church of Jesus Christ of Latter-day Saints,* ed. B. H. Roberts, 2d ed. rev., 7 vols. (Salt Lake City: The Church of Jesus Christ of Latter-day Saints, 1980), 1:64.

6. Ibid., 1:60–61.

7. Charles W. Nibley, in Conference Reports of The Church of Jesus Christ of Latter-day Saints (Salt Lake City: The Church of Jesus Christ of Latter-day Saints, 1898 to present), April 1930, 26–27.

8. D&C 20:1. Based on this scripture, Elder James E. Talmage stated the LDS belief that Jesus was born on April 6, B.C. 1 (*Jesus The Christ* [Salt Lake City: The Church of Jesus Christ of Latter-day Saints, 1982], 96–98; 102–4 in earlier editions). On April 6, 1833, the Prophet Joseph Smith noted that it was "just 1800 years since the Savior laid down His life that men might have everlasting life" (*History of the Church,* 1:337). Elders Orson Pratt, B. H. Roberts, and Charles W. Nibley all agreed (B. H. Roberts, in *Outlines of Ecclesiastical History* [Salt Lake City: Deseret Book, 1979], 17;

Charles W. Nibley, in Conference Reports, April 1930, 26–27).

9. Smith, *History of the Church*, 1:337.

10. Ezra Taft Benson, *Teachings of Ezra Taft Benson* (Salt Lake City: Bookcraft, 1988), 15.

11. The work of translation was a major "branch of his calling" as prophet, and Joseph later testified that the translation was, indeed, a work "which the Lord had appointed" unto him (D&C 76:15; see also *History of the Church*, 1:238).

12. Robert J. Matthews, *A Bible! A Bible!* (Salt Lake City: Bookcraft, 1990), 149–50.

13. Letter from Oliver Cowdery to Phineas H. Young, 23 March 1846, as cited in Larry E. Morris, *A Treasury of Latter-day Saint Letters* (Salt Lake City: Eagle Gate publishing, Deseret Book, 2001), 79.

14. "Conference Minutes," *Times and Seasons*, 5:522–23.

15. "Divine Authority or the Question, Was Joseph Smith Sent of God?" in Orson Pratt, *Orson Pratt's Works* (Salt Lake City: Deseret News Press, 1945), 3, 6.

"PRAISE TO THE MAN"

Brigham Young never tired of praising the name of Joseph Smith. He loved the Prophet and recognized the authority Joseph Smith received to establish the Restoration. President Young said, "I feel like shouting hallelujah, all the time, when I think that I ever knew Joseph Smith, the Prophet *whom the Lord raised up and ordained, and to whom He gave keys and power to build up the kingdom of God on earth and sustain it.* These keys are committed to this people and we have power to continue the work that Joseph commenced, until everything is prepared for the coming of the Son of Man."[1]

Many others have been similarly impressed with the Prophet. Leo Tolstoy, a Russian historian, visited the United States for about a year in 1892 to study the history of great Americans and American institutions. As he was about to board his ship to return to his native land, Tolstoy spoke with Andrew D. White, U.S. minister to Russia, and commented on the genius of the Restoration:

> "I wish you would tell me about your American religion."
> "We have no state church in America," replied Dr. White.
> "I know that, but what about your American religion?"
> Patiently then Dr. White explained to the count [Tolstoy] that in America . . . each person is free to belong to the particular

church in which he is interested. To this Tolstoy impatiently replied: "I know all of this, but I want to know about the American religion. . . . The church to which I refer originated in America and is commonly known as the Mormon Church. What can you tell me of the teachings of the Mormons?"

. . . Dr. White [said], "I know very little concerning them. . . ."

Then Count Leo Tolstoy . . . rebuked the ambassador. "Dr. White, I am greatly surprised and disappointed that a man of your great learning and position should be so ignorant on this important subject. . . . Their principles teach the people not only of Heaven and its attendant glories, but how to live so that their social and economic relations with each other are placed on a sound basis. If the people follow the teachings of this Church, nothing can stop their progress—it will be limitless."

[Tolstoy continued], "There have been great movements started in the past but they have died or been modified before they reached maturity. If Mormonism is able to endure, unmodified, until it reaches the third and fourth generation, it is destined to become the greatest power the world has ever known."[2]

Citing this story in general conference, Elder David B. Haight concluded, "It is not only destined to become, but is the greatest power in the world."[3]

Joseph Smith made a contribution to mankind as great as any theologian, scholar, or politician has made to the world. In 1968, an editor for the *Toronto Star* wrote, "No matter what anyone might think of him, Joseph Smith, the Mormon prophet was one of the most dynamic and creative men of the 19th century. In fact, he is one of a half dozen of the greatest men of that era."[4]

JOSEPH SMITH'S FINAL TESTIMONY OF HIS MISSION

In 1844, when Lucy Mack Smith first saw her sons' (Hyrum's and Joseph's) martyred bodies, she cried out, "My God, my God, why hast thou forsaken this family!" A voice replied, "I have taken them to myself, that they might have rest." She then said, "As I looked on their peaceful, smiling countenances, I seemed almost to hear them say, 'Mother, weep not for us, we have overcome the world by love; we have carried to them the gospel, that their souls might be saved; they slew us for our testimony, and thus placed us beyond their power; their ascendancy is for a moment, ours is an eternal triumph.'"[5]

Thousands attended the funeral of Joseph and Hyrum held in Nauvoo. Later, Brother William W. Phelps paid a final tribute to the Prophet with a poem: "Praise to the man who communed with Jehovah. Jesus anointed that prophet and seer." We might add our own declaration of gratitude: "Praise to Jehovah" and "Praise to the Father" for communing with such great men, including all the prophets of the Restoration.

OUR DAY IN THE HISTORY OF THE CHURCH

Joseph never lived to see Zion completed, but as prophesied, he laid its foundation and he was faithful to his charge (D&C 136:38). Joseph finished his work, but this is now our day in the history of the kingdom of God on the earth. It is up to us to put up the walls and to set the capstone of Zion in place by following the living prophets who hold those same keys Joseph held, and by living the principles of the restored gospel of Jesus Christ.

The Prophet Joseph Smith prayed at the dedication of the Kirtland Temple that one day a Zion-like environment would be created, in which the Savior will be pleased to dwell, and that the Saints would ready themselves, and the world around them, for that special time: "Remember all thy church, O Lord, with all their families, and all their immediate connections, . . . that the kingdom, which thou hast set up without hands, may become a great mountain and fill the whole earth; That thy church may come forth out of the wilderness of darkness, and shine forth fair as the moon, clear as the sun, and terrible as an army with banners; And be adorned as a bride for that day when thou shalt unveil the heavens, . . . that thy glory may fill the earth" (D&C 109:72–74).

Those of us living today have inherited a great legacy. We are the beneficiaries of what the scriptures describe as a "marvelous work and a wonder" (2 Nephi 25:17; 27:26). The worldwide Church of Jesus Christ of Latter-day Saints, organized and established 175 years ago, is indeed the very kingdom of God on the earth. It is the restored Church of Jesus Christ. In our modern world, which seems to be rapidly slouching into secular Sodom and Gomorrah-like conditions, the restored gospel of Jesus Christ is becoming more and more (as prophesied) a "defense, and . . . a refuge from the storm" for millions across the earth (D&C 115:5). It is like an iron rod on the strait and narrow path that leads to Jesus Christ. The gospel of Jesus Christ has been restored that its light may be a "standard for the nations" to look to (D&C 115:5). Joseph noted that there are "many yet on the earth among all sects, parties, and denominations . . . who are only kept from the truth because they know not where to find it—Therefore . . . we should waste and wear out our lives in bringing to light all the hidden things of darkness, wherein we know them; and they are truly manifest from heaven—These should be attended to with great earnestness. Let no man count them as small things; for there is much which lieth in futurity, pertaining to the saints, which depends upon these things" (D&C 123:12–15).

The members of the Church living today have not only inherited a great spiritual legacy but are also expected to shoulder the responsibility to carry this work forward. As President Gordon B. Hinckley further reminded us that we have work to do: "The Lord expects so much of [Latter-day Saints] now because we are not persecuted, we are not driven, we are not on the march, we are not being burned and destroyed and troubled on all sides. We have peace, and we have the good opinion of many, many people in many, many places. How thankful we ought to be and how ambitious we ought to be to move forward this, the work of the Lord."[6]

It is our privilege to stand for the one cause that will emerge victorious! President Hinckley has testified: "This Church is true. It will weather every storm that beats against it. It will outlast every critic who rises to mock it. It was established by God our Eternal Father for the blessing of His sons and daughters of all generations. It carries the name of Him who stands as its head, even the Lord Jesus Christ, the Savior of the world. It is governed and moves by the power of the priesthood. It sends forth to the world another witness of the divinity of the Lord."[7]

Thus, not only will the Church continue to stand, but we have an obligation to stand with it. As Oliver Cowdery was told, "Therefore be diligent; stand by my servant Joseph, faithfully" (D&C 6:18). The Prophet Joseph Smith laid the foundations for this work and it is now up to us to "stand faithfully" until the light of the gospel has penetrated every continent and sounded in every ear. The refreshing rays of the Restoration will give people a greater appreciation for Jesus Christ and His atoning sacrifice and more hope and faith in the future than any other program. We can be optimistic about what will yet transpire, just as President Hinckley has encouraged us to be when he said: "Let us glory in this wonderful season of the work of the Lord. Let us not be proud or arrogant. Let us be humbly grateful. And let us, each one, resolve within himself or herself that we will add to the luster of this magnificent work of the Almighty, that it may shine across the earth as a beacon of strength and goodness for all the world to look upon."[8]

The Prophet Joseph Smith gave his life that we might know how to "come unto Christ" and be perfected in Him. He declared, "God has in reserve a time, or period appointed in His own bosom, when He will bring all His subjects, who have obeyed His voice and kept His commandments, into His celestial rest. This rest is of such perfection and glory, that man has need of a preparation before he can, according to the laws of that kingdom, enter it and enjoy its blessings. This being the fact, God has given certain laws to the human family, which, if observed, are sufficient to prepare them to inherit this rest."[9]

He added, "I think that it is high time for a Christian world to awake out of sleep, and cry mightily to . . . God, day and night. . . . I step forth into the field to tell you what the Lord is doing, and what you must do, to enjoy the smiles of your Savior in these last days."[10]

The Restoration that came through the Prophet Joseph Smith is a declaration of light that will lead us to Jesus Christ, where we can find "peace in this world, and eternal life in the world to come" (D&C 59:23).

Notes

1. Brigham Young, in *Journal of Discourses*, 26 vols. (London: Latter-day Saints' Book Depot, 1854–86), 3:51.

2. *Improvement Era*, February 1939, 94.

3. David B. Haight, in Conference Reports of The Church of Jesus Christ of Latter-day Saints (Salt Lake City: The Church of Jesus Christ of Latter-day Saints, 1898 to present), April 1980, 14.

4. As cited in Jack Jarrard, "Writer impressed with Mormonism," *Church News*, 2 March 1968, 6.

5. Lucy Mack Smith, *History of Joseph Smith by His Mother Lucy Mack Smith* (Salt Lake City: Bookcraft, 1958), 324–25.

6. President Gordon B. Hinckley, at a meeting in Richmond, Virginia, 14 November 1989; as cited in *LDS Church News*, 2 April 2005, 5.

7. Gordon B. Hinckley, "Keep the Faith," *Ensign*, September 1985, 6.

8. Gordon B. Hinckley, "Condition of the Church," *Ensign*, November 2004, 6.

9. Joseph Smith, *Teachings of the Prophet Joseph Smith*, comp. Joseph Fielding Smith (Salt Lake City: Deseret Book, 1976), 54.

10. Ibid., 14.

INDEX

Aaronic Priesthood, restoration of, 119, 122

Abraham, Book of, 101–2, 106

Adam and Eve: apostasy during time of, 20–21; gospel revealed to, 101, 105, 121–22

American Planning Association, 37

Angels, 83–85

Apostasy, Great, 19–20

Apostles: in meridian of time, 20, 80–82; office of, 120

Baptism, restoration of, 89

Baptism for the dead, 113

Benson, Ezra Taft: on Joseph Smith, 52; on fulfillment of 1845 proclamation, 92–93; on great events in history, 123

Bible, Joseph Smith Translation of (JST). *See* Joseph Smith Translation

Bishops, office of, 120

Book of Mormon: ancient prophets know of coming forth of, 78–79, 87–88; lost 116 pages of, 80; translation of, 100–101, 105; completion of, 124

Burnett, Peter H., 60

Cannon, George Q.: on Church resting on revelation, 15; on spiritual education of Joseph Smith, 46; on Joseph Smith as prophet of last dispensation, 53; on Joseph Smith receiving same truths as ancient prophets, 92; on one true gospel, 109

Chiaroscuro, 1

Church members, 9

Church of Jesus Christ (primitive), 19

Church of Jesus Christ of Latter-day Saints: as primitive Church restored, 14, 119–21, 134; growth of, 89, 127–28; as stone cut without hands, 90; is based on revelation, 91–92; final restoration of, 122–24. *See also* Gospel of Jesus Christ

City-design plans, of Joseph Smith, 36–37

Communication, inventions of, 18

Conference Center, LDS, 89–90, 95–96n2

Coray, Howard, 59

Cowdery, Oliver: on Joseph's name being known among nations, 47; receives Aaronic and Melchizedek priesthoods, 73; Moroni shows plates to, 73–74; on organization of the Church, 125–26; standing by

Joseph Smith, 135
Crosby, Jesse W., 28

Daniel, 90
Dark Ages, 19
David, King, 87–88
Deacons, office of, 119
Degrees of glory, 113
Dispensation of the fullness of times, 52–56
Dispensations, other, 21
Doctrine and Covenants, 102–5, 124
Doctrine. *See* Gospel of Jesus Christ
Douglas, Stephen A., 29

Education, 36–37, 62–63
Elders, office of, 120
Elias, 82
Enoch: prophecy of, 4, 101; foresees Book of Mormon, 87–88
Ezekiel, 87–88

Family relationships, 115–16
Faust, James E., 16
First Presidency (1907), 11
First Vision, 14–15, 44
Fisher missionaries, 90
Follett, King, 44

Galland, Isaac, 67n13
Gates, Susa Young, 18
Gathering of Israel, 88, 90
God: is only known through revelation, 21; earthly appearances of, 75–76n9; gospel doctrine on, 114
Gospel of Jesus Christ: Restoration of, 3, 134–35; must go forth to all nations, 4; is constructive to others' beliefs, 8; inventions increase with restoration of, 18; is restored in other dispensations, 21; saving ordinances of, 54; learning principles of, 61; is the same for everyone, 109; restoration of key doctrines of, 110–16; is revealed to Adam and Eve, 121–22
Grant, Heber J., 90–91

Haight, David B., 132
Hancock, Mosiah, 13, 22n1

Harris, Dennison L., 16

Harris, Martin, 71–72, 73–74

Healings, 120

Henrie, William, 73

High Priests, 120

Hinckley, Gordon B.: on strength of Church resting on First Vision, 14; on reverencing Joseph Smith, 42; on Church rolling forth, 91; on Conference Center fulfilling prophecy, 95–96n2; on duties of Church members, 135, 136; on true and living Church, 135

Holy Ghost, 114

Hunter missionaries, 90

Hunter, Edward, 35

Isaiah: knows of Joseph Smith, 78; foresees Book of Mormon, 87–88; foresees Zion, 89–90

Israel, House of, 88

James (apostle), 80–81

James, Jane Manning, 31–33

Jeremiah, 89, 90

Jerome, Saint, 98–99

Jesus Christ: offers his sacrifice in premortal council, 2; enlists Saints in saving mankind, 3–4; invites all to be saved, 10; on coming forth of his work, 17; earthly appearances of, 75–76n9; prophesies of Joseph Smith, 79–80, 81–82; doctrine on, 114; birth and death of, 123, 128n8

John (apostle): knows of Joseph Smith, 80–81; parchment of, 101, 105, 106

John the Baptist, 82, 101

Johnson, Benjamin, 28

Johnson, John, 75n9

Joseph of Egypt, 77–78

Joseph Smith Translation of the Bible (JST), 102, 106, 124–25

Keys, priesthood, 48, 55–56

Kimball, Heber C., 55

Kingdom of God: proclamation on, 55–56, 92–93; prophecy on temporal, 94–95

Kirtland Temple: Christ and God the Father appear in, 76n9; dedication of, fulfills prophecy, 79; dedication of, 134

Lambert, Mary Alice Cannon, 34

Lamp, story of, 5–8

Languages, Joseph Smith studies, 36
Lee, Harold B.: on work of Joseph Smith, x–xi; prophecy of, on raising righteous children, 94; on beginning of the gospel on earth, 116–17n3
Light, borrowed, 9
Lightner, Mary Elizabeth Rollins, 71–72

Mace, Wandle, 61, 70
Malachi, 78–79
Marsh, Thomas B., 74
Matthews, Robert J., 124
Maxwell, Neal A., 2
McConkie, Bruce R., 104–5, 120–21
McConkie, Joseph Fielding, 85
Melchizedek Priesthood, restoration of 119, 122
Micah, 89–90
Missionary work, 90
Morely, Isaac, 75n9
Moroni: appearances of, to Joseph Smith, 45–46, 47, 84; warns Joseph of opposition, 49; on Joseph being held in honor, 51; shows plates to three witnesses, 73–74, 124
Moses: sees Jesus Christ, 45; knows of Joseph Smith, 78; visions of, 101, 105–6
Moses, book of, 101, 105–6

Napoleon, 116–17n3
Nauvoo, 36–37
Nauvoo Legion, 37
Nephi, 87–88, 89
Nephites (at Christ's resurrection), 79
Nero, 19
Nibley, Charles W., 123
Noah, 101, 106
Noble, Joseph Bates, 46

Page, John E., 30
Palmer, James, 70
Parents, righteous, 94
Patriarchs, office of, 120
Pearl of Great Price, 101–2
Persecution, 49–50, 80
Peter, 19, 80–81
Phelps, William W., 133

Phippen, James W., 34–35

Plan of salvation. *See* Salvation, plan of

Pratt, Orson, 91, 26–27

Pratt, Parley P.: on Joseph's testimony in Philadelphia, 5; on charisma of Joseph Smith, 25; on integrity of Joseph Smith, 28; on doctrine of eternal families, 115–16

Premortal existence: council in, 2; doctrine of, 113

Priesthood: authority of, 42; keys of, 48; restoration of, 88–89, 122; sealing power of, 114

Priests, office of, 119

Prophet, the, ix, 42–43. *See also* Smith, Joseph, Jr.

Prophets: speak words of God, 10; office of, 120

Prophets, ancient: know of Joseph Smith, 77–83; Joseph Smith knows, 83–85; prophesy of Restoration, 87–95

Quincy, Josiah, 29

Quorum of the Twelve Apostles (1844–45), proclamation of, 55–56, 92–93

Restoration: as miraculous, 16–17; comes through revelation by God, 41–42; ancient prophets know of, 87–95; of keys doctrines of gospel of Jesus Christ, 110–16; through Joseph Smith, 122–23, 125; of Church of Jesus Christ, 122–24

Resurrection, 114

Revelation: Church rests on, 15, 113; Saints acceptance of, 64–66; Restoration based on, 91–92; as means of gaining scripture, 101–6; on afterlife, 103–4

Richards, Jane Snyder, 33

Richards, LeGrand P., 97, 121

Rigdon, Sidney, 126

Saints (in Joseph Smith's day), 64–66

Salt Lake City, Utah, 36–37

Salvation, plan of: restoration of knowledge of, 110–111; scriptural references to, 112–14

Sampson–Davis, Priscilla, 99–100

Scripture, 97

Sealing power, 114

Seventy, office of, 120

Smith, Asael, x

Smith, Bathsheba W., 34

Smith, Emma Hale: on Joseph Smith talking to men in the garden, 27–28;

helps out Jane Manning James, 31–33; on Joseph Smith's education, 101

Smith, George Albert, x–xi

Smith, Hyrum, 85

Smith, Joseph, Jr., life of: testifies before congregation in Philadelphia, 5; calms militiamen, 25–27; integrity of, 28; influence of, 29, 51–52; love and kindness of, 29–33; first impressions of, 33–34; physical appearance of, 34; has great love for children, 34–35; generosity of, 35; educational and government accomplishments of, 36–38; burial site of, 42; spiritual education of, 43–49; persecution of, 49–50, 80; as prophet of the last dispensation, 52–56; as brilliant thinker and speaker, 59–60; spiritual confirmation by others of, 69–75; is known by ancient apostles and prophets, 77–83; knows ancient prophets and apostles personally, 83–85; fulfills ancient prophecies, 88–89; is appointed by God as translator, 97–98, 100, 128n8; brings forth new scripture, 100–6; restores Church of Jesus Christ, 122–23; praises of, 131–36

Smith, Joseph, Jr., teachings of: on timing of building up of Zion, xii; on purposes of God being accomplished, 11; on Restoration adding to light people have, 11–12; on his own imperfections, 15–16; on passing of priesthood keys to apostles, 48; on destiny of the Church, 49, 134; on being persecuted, 50; on learning principles of Gospel, 61–62; on seeking all types of knowledge, 63–64; on accepting revelation and counsel, 64–66; on testimonies of truth, 69; on prophecies of last days, 87; on fulfilling Daniel's prophecy, 90; on Book of Mormon, 101; on the Bible, 102; on gaining confirmation of truth, 103; on revelation on afterlife, 103–4; on plan of salvation, 111; on eternal families, 115; on beginning of gospel on the earth, 117n3; on comprehending things of God, 121; on Restoration, 134–35; on obtaining God's rest, 136

Smith, Joseph, Sr., x, 49–50

Smith, Joseph F., 9, 93

Smith, Joseph Fielding, 65

Smith, Lucy Mack: on Joseph Smith confounding militiamen, 25–27; on Joseph Smith speaking of ancient Nephites, 84; is comforted on death of her sons, 133

Smith, William, 50

Smucker, Samuel, 29

Snow, Lorenzo, 28, 82

Somerville, William, 35

Sophronius, Eusebius Hieronymous (St. Jerome), 98–99

Spirit world, 113

Spiritual experiences, 69–75

Stevenson, Edward, 73–74

Talmage, James E., 5–8, 128n8

Taylor, John: on Joseph Smith's continuing contributions to world, x; on sharing the light of the gospel, 8; on Joseph knowing ancient prophets and apostles, 46–47, 85; on Joseph Smith as prophet of Restoration, 82–83; prophesies on future of Zion, 93–94; on temporal kingdom of God, 94–95

Teachers, office of, 119

Temple building, 79

Tolstoy, Leo, 37, 131–32

Translation: is gift of God, 97–100, 128n11; works of, 100–6

Transportation, inventions in, 18

Urim and Thummim, 100–101, 105

Wells, Daniel H., 45

Wells, Emmeline Blanch, 33–34, 70–71

White, Andrew D., 131–32

Whitmer, David, 73–74

Whitmer, Peter and Mary, 123–24

Whitney, Newel K., 80

Whitney, Orson F., 14, 95

Winters, Mary Ann, 72–73

Witness, 81–82

Witnesses, Three, 73–74, 124

Woodruff, Wilford: records Joseph passing on keys to apostles, 48; on discourses of Joseph Smith, 70; on Joseph Smith as prophet of Restoration, 81; on Joseph bringing forth new scripture, 104

Young, Brigham: on purposes of God, 9; on the main business of the Saints, 11; on great inventions since Restoration, 18; on persecution of Joseph Smith, 49, 50; on listening to Joseph Smith's discourses, 60–61, 70; praises Joseph Smith, 131

Zion: Joseph Smith designs city of, 36; John Taylor's prophecies on, 93–95

Zion's Camp, 37

ABOUT THE AUTHOR

Jeffrey Marsh received a bachelor's degree from the University of Utah and master's and doctorate degrees from Brigham Young University. An associate professor of ancient scripture at Brigham Young University, he has written curriculum material for seminaries and institutes in the Church Educational System. He has also prepared Melchizedek Priesthood lessons and contributed to the new Gospel Doctrine courses of study.

Brother Marsh is the author of nine books, including *His Final Hours* and *The Light Within*. He and his wife, Kathie, have conducted Church history, Holy Land, and lands of the Book of Mormon tours for numerous groups. They live in South Jordan, Utah, and are the parents of six children.